Weaving with Light

GW00776790

PAUL DANE

First Published 2015

ISBN: 1508719691
ISBN-13: 978-1508719694

Cover illustration: Paul Dane © 2015

weavingwithlight@gmail.com

CONTENTS

PREFACE

If you had woken up this morning to find that all your worries and fears had simply vanished. If you felt completely safe and secure, at peace with yourself and everyone you met. If everything around you filled you with a sense of wonder. In your heart you understood that all the things that have ever happened to you; the good, the bad and the indifferent, were entirely necessary to bring you to this moment here and now. And if you knew that from this moment on you would receive everything you require to have a meaningful life, rich with incredible experiences. Then what would you do differently with today, and tomorrow? How would you change your life? How would you behave differently towards yourself and others?

If later today you also discover that you have been given a gift which enables you to reach out and touch just one person each day. So that the next day when they awake, they too will feel those same wonderful feelings and they too will be able to pass your gift on to just one more person each day. Then how do you imagine they might approach their life differently?

If the following day the two of you could reach two more people, and the following day the four of you reached four more people, and so on, then it would take just 34 days for every person on this planet to be touched by your light.

How then do we imagine we would create our world differently? How would we change our behaviour towards each other? How would we change our behaviour towards the planet that brings us life?

1

CONTEXT

This book is about each of us finding lasting peace and happiness in our life, without losing ourself to the cult of materialism which is causing so much harm to our planet. It is about us developing a deeper sense of self awareness; a deeper connection to one another and the world in which we live, without having to adopt any particular form of religious practice or belief system.

When you look over your life's story so far, perhaps you feel calm and positive. You might see a journey where your relationships with yourself and others are always warm and loving. A journey where people treat you with kindness and respect. Perhaps yours has been a deeply fulfilling life, rich in positive, joyful experiences. You might have experienced a world in which you feel as safe and secure with others, as you do with yourself.

Or perhaps you see something different. Your life might be filled with toil and conflict. It might be a battle against a hostile world, filled with hostile people. Money worries assail you, your body is constantly fighting ill health. Your family, if you have one, is volatile and unpredictable, sometimes a source of strength, more often a source of uncertainty, or worse. Your friends are no more than acquaintances who don't understand or care about you.

Most likely you see your story as a mixture of both.

For many of us, at times, life can be a confusing array of seemingly random events which we try to write into some kind of coherent, positive and meaningful order. Some of those events feel good, some of them don't. Sometimes we feel safe and in control, peace reigns temporarily, and we have spontaneous moments of happiness. Other times we feel as if our whole world is falling apart. We are tired, disillusioned and insecure. Everything and everyone appears to conspire against us.

When we feel lost or confused, it might seem hopelessly unrealistic to imagine a life where everything makes perfect sense. A life where we are at peace with ourself and with all around us. However, there are many amongst us on just such a journey, many whose lives are defined by a sense of inner peace and lasting happiness.

For such people, life is a journey of rich experience. A journey that flows from moment to moment. They understand their relationship with themselves and as a result, understand their relationships with one another and the events of their lives. These people have a deep connection to their world and to everything that inhabits that world with them. More than this, they have a profound sense of connectedness with something greater than themselves, or their possessions. You can find them across all walks of life. They might subscribe to any, or no, particular belief system. They live freely and without fear.

This is not a book about philosophy, science or religion, although it touches on all of those things. Nor is it a self-help guide. It will not tell you how to live your life differently. It will invite you to consider the reasons why your life might not be all that you had hoped for. And it will invite you to consider alternative ways of seeing yourself and the world in which you live, in the hope that you might then go on to experience greater meaning and fulfilment in your life.

This is a book about how, in becoming more self aware, we can each come to know ourself as something far greater than the experiences that make up our everyday life. About how, as we develop our sense of self we can start to choose more lasting inner peace and happiness. And how, as we deepen our understanding of self, we can choose a more connected life which flows naturally together with those around us.

It is a book about you and I choosing to live freely, about us letting go of the anxieties and uncertainties that bind us to mediocre lives filled with uncertainty and grey compromise. It is a book about what we imagine ourselves to be and how we hold ourselves back from discovering the deep sense of wonder that lives within each of us. More than that, it is a book about us coming together, to help resolve much of the damage we have done to our physical world. A book about us taking responsibility for the future of our kind and all that share our planet home with us.

My hope is that somewhere within these words you might find something that resonates with you. Something that helps you take just one small step forward, towards the lasting peace and happiness that flow through you. One small step forward towards your rightful place in the magnificent future that we are capable of creating for ourself, for our kind, and for our planet.

That somewhere in these words you might discover a tiny flicker of light, that guides you towards greater self realisation. And that some day soon, you might reach out and share that light with those who continue to live in darkness around you.

1 OUR HUMAN WORLD

In Chapter 1 we look at why the peace and happiness that we do experience in our life, are so often temporary and insubstantial. We see how our biology programmes us for survival, keeping us constantly on the alert for danger. How it is very hard for us to overcome the anxiety and uncertainty that biological programming brings into our life. We then consider whether there might be something more to our existence, and come up with a simple model to help understand what that something more might be.

Towards the end of this chapter and through to the middle of Chapter 3 we will introduce a number of key terms that are widely used through the remainder this book. Where these terms are first explained they have been highlighted in the text, so that you can easily refer back to them if you feel the need.

Pleasures of the flesh

For some of us, our attempts to find peace and happiness start and end with the body. This approach makes sense, as our body provides us with a vast array of sensations, many of which can be immensely pleasurable.

Every day we are blessed with a stunning array of physical experiences from which we can choose to take pleasure. From music to dance, from the tastes of our favourite food to the smell of delicate flowers. From the shapes and colours of a glorious sunset to a lovers gentle caress. The gifts of our body are compelling and can be beyond compare.

However, the information that our body senses has other important functions too. It enables us to gain the sustenance we need for survival and to respond to potential hazards that might threaten us. Of all these functions our body's 'bottom line' instinct is to look out for dangers to it's physical well being. To deal with such dangers, like many other higher organisms we are hard wired with a fight or flight survival response.

The fight or flight response may have served us well during the early stages of our evolution, and has undoubtedly contributed to the success of our species. It is easy to imagine how, for early man, roaming across a savannah inhabited by large salivating predators, the decision to run away as quickly and as far as possible, might well have had good survival value. Equally, with a body that places us somewhere towards the middle of the food chain, our ability to react quickly with aggression and violence towards more vulnerable species, will have kept our predecessors well fed.

However, in the modern world, our tendency towards fight or flight does not help us create a peaceful or happy life.

Unfortunately for modern man, the physiological pathways and hormones that mediate fight or flight were designed to cope with the immediate, short term dangers and opportunities that we once faced in the wilds. Dangers which either brought us to a gruesome end or ambled off to feast on some other unsuspecting prey. Opportunities that either fed us, or escaped to live another day. However, most of us seldom, if ever, experience such intense or immediate situations in our life today. Instead, our rewards are more often gained by repetitive, often tedious activity. And we are subject to constant, long lasting and often imaginary difficulties that may persist for days, months or even years. Under such circumstances those same bodily responses that ensured our forefathers survival lead to frustration, worry, anxiety, chronic stress and the many detrimental physical and mental conditions that are thought to be associated with such things.

Despite these negative effects, as a species, we have been extraordinarily successful. We have learnt to use tools, settled and developed technologies that have enabled us to jump literally overnight, in evolutionary terms, from somewhere in the middle of the food chain, to become the planets top predator. With this new status we have also gained the potential to reap untold havoc amongst ourselves and all around.

As far as we are aware, no other species has ever managed to change it's position in the food chain at such an astonishing rate. However, like other organic life, our physical bodies evolve very slowly; over countless generations. So it is no surprise, that our body's biology has not had chance to keep up with our changing status on the planet, or the lifestyles that such position and influence bring us. Very often then, when we seek to find our peace and happiness purely through pleasures of the flesh we are left feeling conflicted, knowing that we have been acting out the basic drives of our primitive cave person biology whilst living in a complex digital age.

Equally, if we decide that we cannot find lasting peace and happiness in the sensations that our body offers, and we wish to seek solace in something more, our body's senses appear unable to provide us with information about anything outside of the physical realm in which they exist. As compelling as our body's story is, that which it perceives tends only to be on a scale and of a nature that has utility for our physical survival. Most of the time, our senses reveal nothing more than a working reality heavily skewed towards detecting and acting upon potential threats, feeding and mating opportunities.

Despite appearances, the information we do receive from our senses reveals very little of the physical world in which we live. Our eyes see less than 1% of the available electromagnetic spectrum and many other creatures are capable of detecting things which remain completely hidden from us. For example, bees are able to see light in the ultra violet spectrum. Bats and dolphins shape their world from sound frequencies 7 times higher than anything we can hear. Dogs are believed to have a sense of smell up to 10,000 times more sensitive than our own. Whilst moths can detect pheromones, odourless to us, at distances of over 11 kilometres.

Our bodies also suffer from decay. We cannot avoid the ageing process, and our attempts to escape pain or illness are often unsuccessful. So, if we do seek more lasting peace and happiness in our life, then at some point we might choose to be realistic about how our body can and can't help us. Certainly our body can enable us to experience an amazing physical world filled with an abundance of sights, sounds, tastes, smells and feelings. Certainly it can offer us immensely pleasurable sensations which we can choose to enjoy in the moments that we are capable of participating in them.

However our pleasures of the flesh can only be a fleeting joy. Perhaps all the more exquisite for their fragile transience. They are something for the now and if we become entrapped in our quest to find them, as time passes, we will likely become more and more frustrated by our growing inability to enjoy their experience.

If we wish to find more lasting peace and happiness in our life, then we might choose to look beyond our body.

Beautiful minds

As our body can only provide passing moments of pleasure, we might choose to look to our mind to offer something deeper and longer lasting.

We believe that our mind makes us different. Whilst our bodies have been left behind by our evolutionary leap, our minds have developed far more quickly. Our minds have helped us flourish regardless of our physical limitations. They enable us to do more than simply live out our body's fears and urges. They allow us to self regulate, to work together with one another and with other species.

Most of us believe that our mind is something that originates from incomprehensibly elaborate nerve pathways in our brain. The brains scope is immense with many claiming it contains 'As many cells as there are stars in the Milky Way'. These cells do an amazing job; handling in excess of 2,000,000 inputs each waking second, sorting them out, and determining what to respond to. However, if our mind does reside in our brain it does not generally immerse itself in this massive flow of stimulation. Instead, it involves itself primarily with thought.

Popular belief about the minds ability to think is truly remarkable. With statements like '100,000,000,000,000 ways to think in one instant' and 'more possible thoughts in a lifetime than the number of atoms estimated in the known universe', being common.

The complex nerve pathways, that might give rise to mind are not likely to be fixed and rigid. Like other nerve pathways they are most likely plastic; able to reconfigure in response to the changing needs of our body. Many scientists also believe that attributes such as emotion, which were once thought to come from a mind based predominantly in our brain, actually arise from, and are moderated by, far more complex nerve and hormonal pathways involving our brain, our heart and even our gut.

Because our mind's physical home is so poorly defined and it's output so much less tangible than that of our body, mind itself is very difficult to investigate. Our scientists struggle to understand what mind is, where it comes from and what it is capable of.

We believe that our human mind makes us different from other primates, in some very positive ways. For example, if you put 100 chimpanzees from different family or social groupings into a room and shut the door, the results would be carnage. Whereas generally, if you were to do the same with humans they might mingle freely, sharing thoughts and ideas. Whilst chimps are our closest biological neighbours, we do not consider their minds to be as highly developed as our own, hence we believe them unable to work together in anything more than small social units. Beyond these units we imagine their behaviour to be driven by little more than their body's basic need for survival and procreation. In contrast, although our basic bodily functions are much the same as a chimps we believe that our human mind brings us an unprecedented ability to support the common good and to peacefully co-exist together.

Our mind brings us the ability to delay our body's automatic response to external stimuli. It enables us to hold the moment and consider the likely outcomes of imaginary scenarios. More than this, it interacts with our body to shape the sounds and actions that enable us to communicate with one another, and so accomplish those complex tasks that we would be incapable of achieving alone.

That is only the beginning. Our mind brings us a concept of self, of identity and individuality. It acts as a gateway for elaborate, abstract thought and enables us to manifest countless forms of creativity. We are masterful creators of literature, of the visual arts, of music, of performance, of tastes, of smells, of buildings, of machines and of so much more. Our mind brings us personal meaning, a sense of richness, delightful thoughts and an endless plethora of positive ideas that we might choose to act upon or share with others. Many believe that the mind is also the source of the many emotions which we use to bring depth, richness and intensity to our life.

Our mind brings us so many wonderful gifts that it might appear the perfect place to seek lasting peace and happiness. Particularly as many believe that, in our natural state, our mind makes us truthful, honest and sincere.

However, things are not quite so simple.

The concept of a separate mind and body is misleading. In our everyday life mind and body appear almost inseparable. This linkage is very important to us. If the mind could not take control of many of our body's functions then it's accomplishments would be nothing more than abstract ideas stuck deep inside our physical form. We would have no means of communication, no mechanism by which we could work effectively together and no way to give life to our higher creative thoughts.

In reverse, our body's influence over our mind can be far more problematic: We believe that our mind is dependent on our body's senses to provide it with the information it craves to generate thoughts and ideas. But as we have seen, our cave person body focuses on experiencing a very limited sub set of information, which is mainly geared towards physical survival in a potentially hostile world.

In the same way that our body wants to do whatever it can to survive, our mind also needs us to keep our body intact. So whilst we might be perfectly capable of being truthful, honest, sincere, caring and cooperative, when challenged, our mind, like our body, has a predisposition towards fearing the worse. To compound the situation, our primitive body and hence our mind, wherever it may reside within us, is awash with biology that is in a constant state of readiness, awaiting the next vital threat.

This is why our best intentions can very quickly default to thoughts of survival when anything new or unexpected happens. That survival instinct can drive us to act in fearful and aggressive ways, at the slightest hint that something might not be right in our world.

Whilst our mind might be more capable of offering us moments of peace and happiness than our body, unfortunately it remains enslaved to that body, and is therefore vulnerable to all of those fears and anxieties that hold us back. So if we wish to find more lasting peace and happiness in our life, then at some point we might need to look beyond both our mind and our body.

But before we do that, lets take a look at some of the ways in which the biology of our mind and body plays out, as we go about our everyday life.

Playing it out

As we have seen, only a small proportion of us live in mortal danger or have to capture and kill our own food. However, our body and mind are perfectly built for survival in a hostile, physical world. It makes evolutionary sense for our primitive body to tell us, and for our mind to agree, that we live in dangerous times, because by imagining this we believe we are always ready to keep ourself physically safe.

It is therefore natural for us to live in a state of anxiety. It is also natural for us to fear that if we admit such things to others then somehow we will appear weak and even more vulnerable. We fear that showing our vulnerability might disadvantage us so much that we might no longer be acceptable to others. We fear that if we no longer fit in we might lose those things we hold dear. So, many of us find it very hard to admit, even to ourselves, how deeply we are influenced by insecurity, uncertainty and doubt. However, fear is not a weakness, nor a reason for judgement. It is simply an outcome of the physical journey that we have taken as a species, and it has served us well.

In denying the fear that drives our everyday life we become deeply conflicted and allow it to creep silent and unseen into every aspect of our behaviour. This inner conflict, and the unhappiness that it generates, can be seen in so many ways.

For example, in the well developed world, most of us have sufficient resources to live in reasonable comfort. On the face of it, there is nothing to feel conflicted about and life is good. Yet the statistics regarding anxiety, depression, stress related illness and suicide show how many of us remain deeply unhappy with our privileged lives. We turn to alcohol, nicotine, recreational and prescribed drugs for escape. Whilst this approach can work, it provides only temporary relief. When the drugs wear off, we are left with ourself much as we were before we consumed them. Worse still, this strategy often leads to negative physical, social and economic outcomes that make us even less happy.

Another example of how we try to find happiness in our conflicted lives is the way in which we immerse ourselves in the cult of materialism. So many of us revel in the distraction of buying more and more goods. Often we imagine that if we possess enough 'stuff' we might elevate our status sufficiently to feel safe. Again this approach can work, but provides only temporary distraction. Once the novelty of a new possession has worn off, we are left with ourself much as we were before we bought it. Worse still, if we rely on the acquisition of goods to provide us with comfort, we become trapped in a lifestyle which requires larger and larger amounts of money to support it. In our imagined hostile world, we soon come to fear that we might lose the ability to pay for all the 'stuff' we have come to believe we need. We are stuck in a vicious cycle; the more we fear, the more we need, the more we need, the more we fear.

Looking at our behaviour as a species then, we are clearly neither peaceful nor happy. Yet it seems that the underlying reason we cannot find lasting peace and happiness is simply because we are not made for such things.

Making a choice

All that we have discussed so far is played out by our human self living out our human life in our human world. Our experience of the human world appears bounded by three dimensions and our construct of time. Things that most of us believe to be real. However, if we are destined to have only transient moments of pleasure in our human world, but we sense that life can be so much richer, then perhaps it is time to look beyond our everyday human self and investigate something more.

Throughout recorded history our species has had a concept of something more, which we have shared through our spiritual beliefs. Our spiritual beliefs tend to reflect the needs of the societies into which they were born.

Early beliefs were born of a time when our lives were primarily about survival. We had not developed technology to protect our bodies and we were still very vulnerable to nature. So we bought divinity into nature and all those things that we felt physically vulnerable to. We worshiped the Sun, the Moon, the stars, the earth, water, wind and fire.

Then, as agriculture emerged and more structured societies developed, for some, there were sufficient resources to take time out and ponder more abstract concepts. Time to connect more deeply with whatever forces we felt might shape our world. This led to spiritual beliefs that focused on wider concepts. Such as the nature of the universe and our place within it.

More recently, as populations have grown, and large power structures developed, our spiritual beliefs have been manifest through prophets, with apparent connection to the Divine. Over the years these prophets words have been recorded, often long after death, and used to help structure compliant societies, arguably working towards the collective good in the name of a higher authority.

Whilst our collective belief in something more has evolved with us, the ways in which we express that belief has increasingly fallen foul of the basic fears inherent in our human species. History is littered with acts of cruelty and abuse committed in the name of religion. Of course these atrocities are not related to the something more that religion attempts to connect us to. But to the fears and insecurities of those who seek safety by wielding religious power.

With the advent of science many of us have chosen to wholeheartedly reject the concept of something more. After all, if religion was, and is, the cause of so much injustice then how can anyone claim that 'God is good'?

Yet it is our nature to need something to believe in. So for some, science itself has become a new religion. One that holds fast to a message that, if we cannot measure something in the physical world, then it does not exist. By default then, if something more lies outside of our measurable physical world, then those who follow a religion of science would likely claim that something more can not exist.

However this view empowers science with more truth than it can handle. There are no absolute truths in science, as there are no absolute truths in anything that we experience through our human life. Science is a series of best guesses about some things based on other things that we have previously observed in our physical world. In the same way that scientific truths believed 150 years ago have long been discarded. So shall we discard current scientific knowledge as soon as a better alternative becomes available.

Even with these limitations, science itself is delving deeper and deeper into areas that defy our current concept of a purely physical world. For example, only 50 years ago the ability of two objects to respond to one another instantaneously, across vast distances, with no physical linkage or carrier signal, would have been regarded by most people as pure science fiction. However this phenomenon, known as entanglement, is now widely accepted as a characteristic of matter that we cannot explain with our current scientific knowledge.

There is also a massive body of research and many outstanding scientific minds devoted to investigating examples of something more in action. With fields like; remote viewing, telepathy, psychokinesis, visualisation healing, prescience, shared and near death experience building up a compelling body of evidence and a fascinating array of theories. Of course many of our greatest scientists also have strong spiritual beliefs which they are perfectly able to reconcile with their scientific discipline.

So each of us can make a choice:

Our biology dictates that we are unlikely to experience lasting peace and happiness living out our human life in our human world. However if there is something more then we are unable to touch or measure it using the senses of our body, or normal scientific method. It is therefore a matter of belief. Do we believe that there could be more to life? Or do we believe that those things we can touch, taste, smell, hear, hold and measure are all that there is? In essence, are we happy to live out our mediocre human life, occasionally punctuated by moments of calm and physical gratification. Or is there something within, that tells us we could be so much more?

Something more

Many of us take it as a given that there might be something greater than our human self and the human world we experience. However, some of us are unsure. Perhaps we feel conflicted by the negative impressions that we gain of some religions or their leaders, through our media. Or perhaps we are influenced by the strongly expressed opinions of our family and friends. As we have seen, we might also be confused by science, uncertain how much faith to invest in anything that cannot be validated by physical proof or calculation. Some of us have actively searched for something more, but disappointed at having experienced no definitive eureka moment, have decided to reject the idea.

There are others still, who for their own reasons, simply do not entertain the possibility that there might be anything other than a material world. If that is your strongly held belief right now, then perhaps the remainder

17

of these writings are not for you. However, if you do have a sense that there might be something more, but cannot really identify what it is, or whether it is important to you, then it is time for us to take a closer look at what that something more might be.

There are countless names for something more: The Universe, The Divine, God, Spirit, The Light, Brahman, The Dao, Collective Conscious, One Mind, Love, Source, to name but a few. Depending on our personal preferences, prejudices and background, each of us interprets these different labels in a different way. To avoid aligning with any particular belief system, in this text, we will generally refer to that which lies beyond our human world as simply, the Something More. However, where it fits more closely with the discussion in hand, we may occasionally use any of the other terms interchangeably.

In trying to understand what the **Something More** might be, we immediately run into a challenge. By definition, the Something More is not something that we can directly observe in our human world; it is something more. However, the language that we have at our disposal is largely constructed around the objects and ideas that reside within our human world. So one way we can start to understand what the Something More is, is by describing it with reference to that which it is not. We can also come closer to understanding what the Something More is by direct personal experience, which we will come to later.

The **Something More** is not silent empty space, it is not sky, it is not tree, it is not you, it is not me. It is not matter, or atoms, or all the stars in the universe. It is not anything we can touch, see, hear, smell or taste. It is no-thing we can measure.

The **Something More** is not an object that can be defined by our everyday dimensions of height, width and depth or within the 10 or so dimensions that our mathematicians calculate. Without such dimensions to constrain it, the Something More is therefore omnipresent, infinite and unbounded. It exists within, and outside of, all things that have and ever will be. The Something More is that within which all things become manifest and of which all things are formed. It is the sum of all things through all time, yet within itself it is no-thing, nor is it nothing.

Equally, the **Something More** does not exist within our construct of time. Without time to constrain it, the Something More is therefore both instant and eternal. In the Something More there is no difference between now and eternity. The Something More is the eternal instant within which all time is contained.

The **Something More** is all life, it is all intelligence, it is all thought, all experience, all hopes, all dreams and all fears. It is all experiences of itself, yet of itself it is none of these things, they are all simply an aspect of it.

Of itself, the **Something More** is too great a concept for the human mind to comprehend or explain. So, many of us personify our relationship with the Something More in the form of deities. Or choose to experience it as spirits and other mystical phenomenon.

As we have no way to truly understand what the **Something More** is, then anything we personify it to be, is entirely possible. Who is to say that my deity is any different from, or more real than yours? Equally, whatever we personify the Something More to be, that personification is simply another layer of human construct, contained ultimately within the Something More. It is not a description of what the Something More truly is.

The **Something More** is not just around us, it is not simply something that we believe in or not. It is all that we are, it is all that we will ever conceive and it is all that we shall ever experience in our human world.

Awareness and our highest self

Most of the time, we imagine we have no choice but to live out our human life, bound to the uncertainties, insecurities and occasional joys of our biological existence. However, this is not the case. We have a key that enables us to slip away from the bonds of body and mind. And we have a gateway through which we can pass to experience greater things.

Our key we will call self awareness. To understand self awareness we must first imagine a greater concept. This greater concept we will simply call awareness. **Awareness** is that aspect of the Something More that contains and connects the experience of all things that have and ever will exist, including ourselves. How it does this we don't need to know, and we probably never will. Because the process, if there is one, is that which enables us to create our human experience and is not therefore something that exists *within* our human experience. Awareness flows constantly within and between ourselves, as it flows within and between everything else that we experience in our life. It is the life force that flows into us at conception and then withdraws on death. As such, awareness might be similar to what you have already come to know as soul, spirit or chi, if you choose to believe in such things.

Self **awareness** is that unique part of awareness that makes you, *you*. It is that small spark within that chooses to experience *your* unique life: As awareness contains all possible sensations of the body, so *your* self awareness chooses to feel the sensations that *you* feel in the moment. As awareness contains all possible thoughts of the mind, so *your* self awareness chooses to listen to the thoughts that *you* think in the moment. Self awareness is the creative force which chooses to experience all that you imagine yourself to be, in the instant of now. It is that which makes *your* life different to any other. As such, self awareness might be similar to what you have already come to know as consciousness.

For most of our waking life, our **self awareness** sits mainly with our mind. For example, if you think about your work it most likely involves solving problems, using equipment or doing other things that involve mental activity. Even when you are on 'auto-pilot', such as driving your car, you are still likely to be thinking about things; the day ahead, your recent activities or a personal issue that you are struggling to resolve. If you go to the supermarket, take a trip on the tube, or walk down a busy street, you only need raise your gaze and look directly at others, to observe how entrapped in our thoughts most of us are, most of the time. However, although our self awareness spends most of its waking time sitting with our mind, it is not tied to that mind. We all have experiences when our self awareness is very much in our body, perhaps through exercise, intimacy or pain. We also have experiences when our self awareness connects to our body in more subtle ways, such as when we are enjoying the sights and sounds of art and music.

Because **self awareness** is a part of awareness and awareness constantly flows through all things, self awareness is not tied to our human form. This means that although most of us, most of the time, only choose to experience the mind and body that make up our human self, we are all free to experience other things outside of our human self, as and when we choose.

The ability of self awareness to choose experiences outside of mind and body might be challenging for some

21

to accept. However, many are familiar with the concept. After all, where do we imagine we 'go to' when we are asleep or if we become unconscious? For those with an interest in practices such as yoga or meditation, the idea that our self awareness can move beyond the confines of mind and body is probably quite familiar.

As self awareness is free to choose experiences beyond our human self, it is able to approach our gateway to the Something More. A gateway that we will call our highest self.

We can imagine our **highest self** as that which connects our human self to other aspects of the Something More, that exist outside of our human world. On one side, our highest self understands our human fear, uncertainty and doubt. On the other, it knows that we are so much greater than any of those things that we can experience or even conceive, in our human world.

Our **highest self** knows our capacity to manifest beauty. It is a subtle voice that constantly whispers our highest concept of that which we are, that which we can choose to experience and that which we can become. Our highest self knows how and why we live our human life in the way we do. As it knows how and why we might come to shine with the pure light of the Something More, as and when we are ready.

It is the ability of self awareness to move beyond the limitations of our human self and to approach our highest self that at last sets us free to choose lasting peace and happiness in our life.

Whilst most of us would accept that we are self aware, some might struggle with concepts such as the Something More, awareness and highest self. If that is your situation right now, then you don't need to get too lost in the words.

Those words are simply here to build a model that helps us understand something beyond words. It is not the specific structures that we build into the model, or the words that we use to describe those structures, that matter. What matters, is how we can take the model, reshape it to fit with our own, current, world view and then use it to bring greater meaning and understanding to our life experience.

Feeling trapped?

One of our challenges in coming to accept that we might be more than our purely human self is that for so many of us, all we know, and all we have ever known, is our human world. Awareness and self awareness do such a magnificent job and choose such compelling experiences for us that we become entrapped in our human life.

Whether we are immersed in the pursuit of wealth, security, status or pleasure, our life experience is rich, immediate and relentless. Each day we use up all of our energy trying to hold on to the things that we desire and trying to come up with new ways to get more. There is nothing intrinsically wrong with experiencing our life in this way. However, for the reasons we have seen, entrapped in the human world, it is all too easy for us to believe in the fears, uncertainties and doubts that make us so unhappy.

In our human world, no matter how hard we might try to hold on to friends and family, we know they are ultimately free to make their own decisions and can choose to leave us at any time. No matter how much wealth or power we might accumulate, in the face of the universe, we ultimately believe ourself to be nothing more than a small speck of matter, desperately clinging to a temporary, fragile existence. Worse still, entrapped in our human world we come to believe that our incredibly short, vulnerable, and ultimately insignificant human life is the be all, and end all, of all that we can ever be. Not surprisingly then, entrapped in our human world some of us might come to question whether there is any point in having a human life at all.

However, our highest self knows that we are so much greater than the human reality that our self awareness chooses to experience through our mind and body. It knows its relationship with the Divine and therefore knows its immortality. As we will see, our highest self delights in *all* of the experiences that we choose for our self, whether we choose to judge those experiences as good or bad.

So again we can make a choice. We can choose to remain entrapped in our human life, accepting those fleeting moments of peace and happiness as our lot. Or we can choose to develop our concept of self. We can choose to conceive our existence as something greater than our human self, living out our human life in our human world. We can choose to conceive a life where our self awareness shakes free from the bonds of our mind and body and starts to experience the true wonder of our highest self.

If we choose to free our self awareness, then we might imagine that our life could be less fulfilling. That perhaps in coming to know our highest self, with one foot in the human world and one foot in the Something More, our experiences might become somehow diluted. After all, if all we have ever known is the human world, then when we experience that world, aren't we truly 'in it'? But if we know that our human world is not so important, because at our core, we know we are a part of something so much greater, then doesn't everything feel a little pointless?

Quite the opposite is true.

In becoming more self aware we do not diminish the experience of our human life. We come to know ourself to be *more than* our human life. We gently release those insecurities and frustrations that drained our energy and held us back. In their place we find a deep calm and certainty that enable us to experience everything that our life brings, more fully. We allow the walls that we have built around ourself to crumble, the worries that have exhausted us to fade.

Far from dulling our life experience, such knowing and the peace it brings, enable us to fearlessly immerse ourself in truly living. The most simple natural experiences bringing massive enrichment. The colours of a sunset, the wind in the trees or the sound of bird song can carry us on waves of intense pleasure, incomparable with the latest acquisition or conquest that we previously strove for in our purely human life.

2 IMAGINING THINGS DIFFERENTLY

In Chapter 2 we look at some of the reasons why the ideas we came up with in Chapter 1 make sense. We go on to explore how our life experience is shaped around two basic agreements which put each of us at the centre of our own personal reality. Then we look at how, by understanding these agreements, we can empower ourself to start creating more lasting peace, happiness and fulfilment in our life.

If the ideas in Chapter 1 sit comfortably and make complete sense to you, and if you are more interested in exploring how a greater concept of self can help you deal with the challenges of everyday life, then at this point, you might choose to skip straight to Chapter 3 'Working it out'. You might also choose to skip straight to Chapter 3 if, right now, you feel uncomfortable dealing with seemingly abstract concepts such as the nature of reality and our part in creating it together. In which case, perhaps you might choose to come back to this chapter later.

You expect me to believe that?

Entrapped in our human world, many of us believe that our reality is made up entirely of material objects which exist in a physical universe. We also believe that physical universe and the objects within it change, dependent on a 'dimension' which we call time.

This view might particularly appeal to you if you have a strong grounding in materialism, or a leaning towards science and technology. Most likely you have felt very little need to question whether such a concept of reality really serves you very well, or has any true validity. However, seeing reality in this way, we have very little chance to move beyond our entrapment in the human world. Equally, our belief in a solid, external reality, bounded within time, does not stand up very well to scrutiny. For example:

Take a look at the nearest wall. If I ask you what that wall is made of, you might reply with an answer like 'bricks and mortar', 'wood' or some other material. If I then ask you what that material is made up of, you might answer 'chemicals', 'molecules' or something similar. If I ask the same question again, you might come up with 'elements' or 'atoms'. If I ask the question one more time, then you might pause. Perhaps, if physics is a field that interests you, you might start to try and explain a whole zoo of sub atomic particles or mathematical concepts to me. Some of which are entirely theoretical, and most of which are very difficult for the lay-person to understand. You might also volunteer that, in truth, there isn't really very much of anything actually 'in' that wall at all. Because, for a typical atom like Hydrogen, 99.9999999999996% is empty space.

So, if all of those objects that make up our physical universe are at least 99.999999999999% empty space, then how 'real' are those objects really? And how real, can the universe that we believe contains them really be?

Delving deeper, if I then changed the subject slightly and said: 'Well OK, tell me how much of the universe is made up of these atoms and sub-atomic particles, that I am trying to understand?' Again, if you had an interest in physics, you might come up with an answer like 'Well… about 4%…but we've only observed half of that'.

The remaining 96% of what we believe to comprise our physical universe is known as dark matter and dark energy.

Right now, we have no conclusive agreement whether dark matter and dark energy are the same, or different things. They have never been observed, we don't know where they come from and we don't know what they are. However, we are told that dark matter and/or dark energy must exist for our scientific observations and calculations to hold true.

We also believe that our entire life experience exists within a 'dimension' that we call time. Without time, we imagine no events would ever happen. We would not be born, we would not age, we would not die. We would be unable to speak, think, or learn. We would not have children, and we would not be able to create, lose or destroy anything. Without time, we believe, there would be no past and no future. We believe that absolutely nothing could happen in our human world without time.

However, for all their endeavours, our philosophers and scientists still have no definitive agreement about what time actually is. Depending on who you ask, you might be told that time is a constant, measurable dimension. Or you might be persuaded that time is something which varies massively, dependent on other physical criteria, such as the relative speed at which an object is moving. Others might tell you that time is a largely subjective phenomenon that exists simply because it has to, 'to keep everything from happening at once'.

So, given that scientists tell us we can only see and measure around 2% of what we believe 'must' be in our physical universe, and of that 2%, more than 99.999999999999% appears to be absolutely nothing at all. And given that, although we believe time to be so important in our lives, we still have no consensus about what it might be, or whether it even exists. How plausible is our commonly held belief that reality might be no more than material objects which exist in a physical universe and change with time? How many gamblers would base their life decisions on such flimsy odds?

Many of us intuitively sense that reality must be something greater than the material objects that we imagine define our existence. Often coming up with comments like 'well it's all just energy anyway, isn't it'. This view helps us let go of the constraints of a purely physical world. However, again it does not stand up well to scrutiny.

Science currently identifies 9 different forms of energy; chemical, kinetic, gravitational, elastic, electrical, thermal, nuclear, light and sound. Most of these can be converted to one another and all have some kind of relationship with the physical objects we experience in our everyday life. So which energy do we choose to believe creates our reality? And how confident can we be in this choice? Particularly, given that we have already seen 96% of the universe might be composed of dark energy that we cannot observe in any way at all?

Science is an incredibly powerful tool which we can use to understand and manipulate our shared experience of a physical reality. However, the reason why we fail to understand what most of that physical reality really is, is because we do not need that physical reality to exist, for us to experience our human life.

Creating reality

Undoubtedly, most of us do choose to experience our human life as something bounded by three dimensions and the flow of time. But that limited concept of reality is only a very small part of something far greater. The physical reality that we choose to experience in our human life is a 'lesser reality'. Our **lesser, human reality** is a subjective reality, personal to each of us. It is therefore something which each of us is free to experience in our own unique way.

None of us has any way of experiencing another persons version of their **lesser, human reality**. However, as we will see later, there are aspects of our lesser, human reality which we do choose to share. Good examples of such shared aspects are; our commonly held belief that the sky is blue, that the grass is green, that reality is the same for all of us and that it conforms to the laws of science.

Each of us is also a part of a **greater reality**. Our greater reality encompasses all of our different versions of lesser, human reality. However, it also extends into something infinitely more and is therefore far greater than just the sum of all our lesser, human realities put together.

Our **greater reality** is not confined by our personal experience of the human world. It does not conform with, or need to be constrained by the laws of science or man, because those laws are simply a minor component of it. Our greater reality is timeless, infinite and unbounded. It is the realm of the Something More.

Whilst most of us choose to believe that our life experience is shaped by the things that we do in a physical reality 'out there', our life experience is ultimately shaped by the experiences that our self awareness chooses to experience. And all of those experiences which our self awareness might choose to experience are contained within, and connected by, awareness. Because awareness is a part of our greater reality, the life experiences that we do choose for ourself therefore come from the realm of that greater reality, not from the realm of our lesser, human reality.

This means that, it is our self awareness that *chooses* to experience our life as something that exists within a lesser, human reality. As it is our self awareness that *chooses* to experience all of the laws, rules and boundaries that we believe constrain that human reality. It is also our self awareness that chooses to experience our human reality as something filled with external, physical objects which change through time. It is not an external, physical reality or objects changing through time that lead to our experience of being self aware.

A simple way to picture this, is to take two pieces of plain paper. On one you can draw the outline of a person, and label this outline 'Body'. Then draw a circle in the middle of the head area, labelling it 'Mind'. Then a circle in the middle of the mind area, labelling it 'Self Awareness'. Outside the outline of the body that you first drew, you can write 'Physical Reality'. This is how most of us choose to see ourselves within our human world.

On the second piece of paper, draw a random shape, any shape you like. Label this shape 'Mind-Body'. Inside your mind-body write 'Human Reality' and outside your mind-body write 'Greater Reality (Something More)'. Finally, draw a line with an arrow head at each end. Start this line in the human reality area, let it cross the boundary of your mind-body and end up in the greater reality area. Label this line 'Self Awareness'. This sketch depicts how our human reality is something created and bounded by our choice to experience a mind and a body. It shows our greater reality as something that contains our mind and body and therefore contains our human reality. More importantly it shows how our self awareness is unbounded, able to sit in those experiences of mind and body that make up our human reality. But free to sit in our greater reality, touching on the Something More, as and when we choose. Hang on to this second sketch for now, as we will use it again later.

Such ideas might appear academic. However, whilst our awareness of self remains confined within our human reality, we remain bounded and vulnerable to the physical world and all those rules that we choose to believe govern that world. In contrast, if we free our self awareness, and know ourself to be part of a greater reality, we become unbounded, interconnected and safe. In addition, if we understand how our greater reality interacts with the lesser reality of our human world, then we are able to create, experience and share a richer, happier and more meaningful life, in that human world.

For those of us firmly rooted in the material world, it might seem far fetched to suggest that world might not need to be entirely 'real' for us to choose to experience it. However, we all know that our self awareness is perfectly capable of creating compelling experiences of reality for us, without any need for input from an external physical world. Because that is exactly what we do, every day, when we are asleep and dreaming.

There are other reasons why we might believe that we are more involved in creating our own personal reality than most of us imagine. For example, as far back as the 1930's nuclear physicists became aware that the fundamental building blocks of matter, might exist in multiple states simultaneously. Such that, at a human scale, situations could be imagined where objects don't take on any particular form, until an observation of them is made.

Equally, we know that none of us will have any definitive proof about what happens to us after we die, until we are dead. So do we believe that our human world simply carries on without us? Or does it somehow change? Or perhaps it simply disappears, without us being there to experience it? As we cannot answer these questions with any certainty, how certain can we be that there really is a physical reality 'out there' that will last any longer than we do?

Many of us already believe that the things that happen to us can be influenced by things that are not a part of any solid physical reality at all. For example:

There is a popularly held belief that if you approach life with a positive attitude events appear to turn out positively for you. Whilst those we meet who constantly expect the worst, seem to have endless stories about situations which they believe justify their negative opinions. So do bad things keep happening to people who think they will? And do good things keep happening to people who expect them to? Or do different people simply see things in different ways? And regardless of the answer, does it not appear that each person is playing a significant part in creating their own personal version of reality?

In the same way, if we expose two people with different dispositions, to exactly the same event, they often appear to process that event quite differently. One person might see it is as the inevitable outcome of a series of prior events, and experience it with calm acceptance. The other might see it as something unexpected and disappointing, experiencing it with fear and anxiety. One might see it as the perfect opportunity to let go, move on, and do something new with life. The other might see it as time to dig in, fight a battle and get their own way. So, are these two people exposed to fundamentally different experiences? Or are they somehow creating their own unique interpretation of the situation? Either way, doesn't it appear that the personal reality that each of them experiences is fundamentally different and quite likely something that they create within themselves?

We already know that our bodies only detect an infinitesimally small amount of the energy that flows through and around them. We also know that they bring a much smaller sub-set of that energy forward for us to process. And we know that even then, our minds only raise an even smaller group of thoughts to consciousness. So how real is the physical reality that we choose to believe in? Does it really determine all those things that happen to us or do we each have a far greater part to play in how we create the experience of our life?

Understanding our agreements

It might not be as difficult as we imagine for us to create our own reality. This is because, whilst we all imagine our life to be layer upon layer of complexity, awareness and self awareness only require two fundamental agreements to experience and share our human world. All of us sign up to these agreements when we choose to have a life. Because without them, we would have no common foundation on which to build a shared world. And without a shared world, our lives would be greatly diminished.

These agreements are duality and causality.

By understanding how our world is created from duality and causality we are able to let go of the belief that we must be constrained by the many rules that govern our everyday life. In coming to understand how duality and causality work, we are able to make much more sense of the things that we choose to experience in our life. And, by making sense of the experiences that we have in our life, we come closer to finding lasting peace and happiness.

Our agreement of **duality** enables us to create and share, experiences of material objects. It is about the experience of opposites. About one experience not existing, without it's opposite also being in existence. Duality determines that we cannot know light without knowing dark. We cannot know hard, without knowing soft, we cannot know hot, without knowing cold and we cannot know anything without knowing its absence.

When our self awareness chooses the experience of a human life, it is actually choosing to experience a unique flow of **duality**; things like happiness and sadness, sound and silence. It is choosing to blend experiences of duality such as dark and light, to create shade, or hot and cold, to create warmth.

We are masters at subtly interweaving complex **dualities** to create the differences between the myriad things that we experience in our human life. It is not difficult for us to create, blend and interweave dualities in this way because, after all, we choose to experience a human life in which we are blessed with the perfect tools to do just that. We choose a human body, intricately designed to generate experiences of sensory **duality**, and a human mind perfectly fashioned to generate experiences of duality in thought and feeling.

In our human world, we cannot do anything other than experience **duality**. For example; if I look at an oil painting, I experience a set of dualities which include light and dark, texture and smoothness and the presence and absence of colour. Likewise, if I listen to a piece of music, I choose to experience a set of dualities that include the presence and absence of sound.

Even if I put my scientific hat on and choose to investigate the physical properties of the music that I have just listened to, I simply go on to create further experiences of duality. For example, the movement or stillness of a needle on a dial, or the presence and absence of a flashing light on some measuring equipment.

From those dualities, I might decide to agree with the idea that music is composed of something we collectively know as sound waves, or I might not. However, regardless of whether I choose to measure that music, and regardless of whether I choose to agree with the idea that music is composed of sound waves or not, I am entirely able to experience it to the full, through its' subtly blended and interwoven dualities.

Equally, because **duality** is a fundamental agreement that my self awareness and your self awareness sign up to when we choose to experience a human world together, I can choose to share any of my experiences of subtly blended and interwoven duality with you, in a meaningful way. As you can choose to share yours with me.

We know dualities are real because we experience them all of the time. Reading this book you are experiencing dualities right now; in the differences between the light and the dark of the words on the page. If you walk over to touch the wall that you were looking at earlier, you know it is real, for you, because of the dualities of softness and hardness that you experience as your hand passes through the air and then pushes against it.

The fact that duality determines we cannot experience anything without the experience of it's opposite also existing somewhere in the human world, has profound implications for both ourselves and for our species.

At a personal level, if we understand duality, then we understand, and can come to accept that our life might go through some very different phases. At one time we might choose a busy, active life, filled with opportunity and friendship. However, duality dictates that if we choose such things for ourself, then there will be other times when we choose a stagnant life. Times when we feel alone and devoid of hope. During those down times, many of us might blame ourself for 'losing the plot', 'being weak' or being 'unworthy'. Or we might blame others for contributing to our change in circumstances. We might start to imagine ourselves as victims.

However, if we understand duality, we can come to accept that life will have it's ups and downs; it cannot be otherwise. We find peace in the knowledge that the dark periods we experience are the inevitable opposites of the times when the sun shines for us. Equally, we come to know that as we experience the lows in our life, so shall we experience the highs. If we understand duality, then when life is difficult for us we no longer need to make ourself sad or angry. We can simply accept the situation with peace and calmly put our energies into dealing with our challenges.

Duality also works on a far larger scale: There is massive disparity in the way that money is distributed amongst us; with 1% of the population now controlling nearly half of the worlds wealth. The top 85 richest people on the planet have as much wealth as the poorest 3.5 billion. Most of us believe this to be wrong and believe it to be a cause of great suffering. Whilst a lot of people put a lot of effort into attempting to redistribute resources to the poor, many also feel that, in the face of such massive disparity, our attempts to bring relief are almost futile. However, understanding duality we see that it is inevitable that if a small number of people hold on to a vast amount of wealth, then a vast number of people will have no wealth at all.

Equally, we see that, if that small number of people evolve sufficiently to find peace within themselves, they will realise that no amount of riches will ever make them feel any more happy or secure. If they come to understand that their life would feel so much more meaningful if they released their wealth for the good of the species, then the duality of wealthy and poor would cease to exist, and global wealth would naturally redistribute more equitably.

Of course, this only holds true if *all* of us are sufficiently evolved to know that we do not need to hoard wealth to feel safe in our world. Otherwise the duality will remain and simply continue with new players in new roles. So, whilst we might point our finger at the super rich and blame them for creating massive poverty in the world, we must *all* evolve beyond the belief that hoarding wealth will bring us a happier more meaningful life, if we want the situation to change.

There are also some amongst us who are very driven to seek safety and security by wielding power over others. As a result, of the 7.2 billion people on the planet right now, less than 100 are believed capable of exercising significant influence on the global stage. Again, this creates duality, making it inevitable that vast numbers of us will be voiceless and powerless. As with wealth, this duality will remain until each of us has evolved sufficiently to be at peace with ourself and realise that there is no need to seek safety and security by having power over others. Until we all reach this point, it does not matter what political, commercial or religious structures we put in place, the duality will remain. However, once we do reach this point then the duality of powerful and powerless will end. At which stage, power will naturally redistribute more equitably between all of us and relevant, new, decision making structures will evolve, on a global scale.

As one of only two fundamental agreements in our human world, duality works in even greater ways. It exists in greater forms; such as Yin and Yang, Heaven and Earth, male and female. The principal of duality can be found in teachings many thousands of years old, such as the Dao, and underlies more modern beliefs such as Jung's 'paired opposites'. If we look at popular culture, we can see that many of us already have a sense of the way in which duality works. With sayings like 'no sunshine without rain', 'no pain, no gain', and 'every cloud has a silver lining' revealing our innate understanding of the agreement.

For many of us, causality is much easier to understand than duality. **Causality** is simply about cause and effect. Our agreement of causality dictates that, as we choose an experience of one thing, in our human world, so we automatically go on to choose an experience of the next. Things therefore happen in sequence, one after the other, and whilst we might freely make choices, every one of those choices will lead to new outcomes and new choices.

We have seen how time appears to be difficult for us to understand, without form or substance in the material world. This is because time is not really very important in helping our self awareness experience our human life. It is **causality** that enables us to write the story of our life in sequence. The subjective amount of time between the events that we write into that story, is largely irrelevant.

Causality dictates that when we share experiences with other people, we do not arbitrarily choose to come together at some randomly selected time and just see what happens. Instead, our self awareness determines that the situation is right to interweave the chains of cause and effect that we have each experienced. So that each of us can then go on to experience new chains of cause and effect that will serve us better, and that we could not experience alone.

By understanding causality we understand more fully, how and why things happen to us when they do, and so become more calm and positive about the events we experience in our everyday life.

For example, we often find that things happen much later than we imagine we would like them to. This is because causality dictates that our interactions together are not determined by time, they are determined by our state of readiness. If all parties are not ready to share an experience then nothing can be shared, regardless of time.

For the same reason, sometimes the things that we believe should happen, never do. This is simply because no one is ever truly ready to take part. By understanding causality we know that, on occasions, we must be patient and accept the natural flow of events, rather than continue to push on closed doors. Equally, causality is the reason why sometimes, things which are entirely unexpected, come into being. Such things are, most likely, the outcome of chains of cause and effect, initiated long ago, and far too complex for us to comprehend.

By understanding causality, we know that regardless of immediate outcomes, it can be worth doing the things we believe in. Because eventually they might well evolve and come back to us, or help someone else.

Understanding causality we know we do not need to be alarmed, blame ourself or blame others when we are faced with a challenging new situation. We know that situation might simply be the outcome of actions we took, way back. And that we are better to concentrate on dealing with current events, rather than putting our energy into persecuting ourself or looking for someone else to blame.

As we observe causality at work, we become much better at standing aside and anticipating the outcomes of our actions. We learn what is necessary to do and what is not. In this way our life takes on more direction and flows more peacefully.

Many of us have an innate understanding of causality, with sayings like 'you get what you give' 'one thing leads to another' and 'the end is in the beginning' all touching on the agreement. Like duality, causality has many profound implications and underlies spiritual concepts such as divine justice and Karma.

Understanding duality and causality is so important in our life because, when we only believe in our lesser, human reality, we believe that the material world is so much greater than ourself, and we believe ourself to be ultimately powerless. However, in knowing that our lesser, human reality is simply something that our self awareness chooses to experience, based on our agreements of duality and causality, we become empowered. We understand that, regardless of what we have chosen to experience in our human world right now, we are able to work with those basic agreements to make new choices that serve us better in the future.

If we feel caught in a chain of cause and effect that no longer serves us, we know that we are free to initiate a new chain of cause and effect, either alone or with others, as soon as we are ready, to see if that new chain serves us any better. Likewise, if we are experiencing duality that we no longer want in our life, we know that, as soon as that duality plays out, we are free to let it go, move on, and experience new dualities which are perhaps more peaceful and less extreme.

Most importantly, by understanding duality and causality, we understand that our human life must be bound by these agreements, because without them we would be unable to share our human world together.

However, we also know that because duality and causality are *only* needed for us to share our human world together, then those agreements are not needed beyond the lesser reality of that shared human world. This means that, when we approach our highest self and sit within our greater reality, we are no longer entirely bound by such agreements.

As we sit more closely with our highest self, so we start to free ourself of the complex, uncontrollable outcomes that causality can so often create for us. We free ourself of the roller coaster of highs and lows that duality so often brings into our life.

Getting it together

Of course our human world does have other people in it too, and we must grant others the same creative powers and freedoms that we grant ourself. We must grant them the same capacity to create their own unique life story. We are therefore more than isolated creators of our individual life experience; we are co-creators of our collective human experience.

Co-creation flows subtly between all of us.

For example, there is a beautiful Rowan tree outside my house. In Autumn, it reaches the height of my bedroom window where I can watch it's leaves turn vivid scarlet-red. It often has striking red berries on as well. I have no way of knowing how many clusters of berries the tree will carry each year, or on which branches those clusters will form. So when I look at it and see a collection of berries for the first time, that is the first time that those particular berries exist in my human experience.

The more often I look at those berries, and the more detail I observe, then the more real they become. If I glance casually at them on just one occasion, they quickly slip out of my world. On the other hand, if I spend an afternoon scrutinising them, looking at the shape, colour and location of each berry, then they stay in my experience much longer and become more real. So it is with all that we choose to experience; the more we engage our self awareness with that experience, the more real that experience becomes in our human world.

In the same way, if I was to invite one of my children to come and look at those berries with me, then we would likely agree on some details. 'Look at those berries on the third branch from the bottom, aren't they a lovely shade of red'. Here we are co-creating. Those aspects of the berries that we choose to experience together become more real because they are experienced by the self awareness of more than one person.

Co-creation is very powerful. The more people share the experience of something, the greater that thing becomes, and the more influence it has on our experience of our shared human world together. So, whilst each of us is entirely free to choose our own life experience, that choice can be strongly influenced by the things that we choose to co-create with others.

An easy way to picture how **co-creation** works, is to take the sketch of our greater and lesser realities that you drew earlier. Copy it several times, to represent several people. Then lie the copies one on top of the other. If you make sure that the areas labelled 'Human Reality' roughly line up, then you can take a pencil or something sharp, and push it through all of those lesser, human realities at the same time. By doing this you bind each lesser, human reality together at one particular point. In the same way, co-creation binds our personal human realities together, at, and only at, the points where we choose to share our human life experience.

Co-creation underlies the massive impact that our media has in shaping our human world. If we collectively choose to experience images and stories that play on our innate fears and insecurities, then we collectively choose to share a fearful, insecure human reality. And together, we collectively choose to co-create a fearful, insecure human world. However, if we choose not to expose ourself to such things, then we cease to allow them to influence our life. With no one engaged in a fearful, insecure human world, fear and insecurity will start to leave our collective human experience.

This argument might appear hopefully naive to some. A bit like suggesting an Ostrich that buries its head in the sand is correct in assuming that it will be safe. How could peoples collective choice not to experience something cause it to end? However, most of us would accept that, if we cease to watch a certain T.V. channel, or cease to buy a certain product then market forces will soon cause them to disappear. A view which sounds remarkably similar to saying that if all of us choose to stop something being a part of our life experience, then that thing will soon cease to exist.

Co-creation is the reason why the lesser, human realities, that make up our shared human world, are so convincing.

If we go back to the wall we discussed earlier, despite scientific evidence, most of us would probably find it very hard to believe that it could ever be anything other than a solid physical object. This is simply because, so many of us choose to co-create and share the experience of a wall, as something which is solid. And with so many of us choosing to create the experience of a wall as something solid, it is very difficult for any one of us to choose to experience it as anything else.

However there are many experiences that far smaller numbers of us choose to co-create together. For example, some people believe that they have seen ghosts or spirits, others maintain that this is impossible. This is because, whilst concepts like our wall are co-created by many billions of us, such supernatural phenomenon are co-created on a much smaller scale. Hence we experience our wall as something solid and immovable, whilst those who choose to experience ghosts and spirits generally experience such things as flimsy and insubstantial. Of course, for those who do choose to experience the supernatural in this way, those experiences are as real as any other that they might choose to be a part of their everyday life.

The solid wall which we experience so convincingly is simply an experience of the duality of inside and out, that we choose to co-create together. As we saw earlier, from that co-created duality of inside and out, most of us then go on to create further experiences of duality such as hard and soft, light and dark, warm and cool, to bring substance to our experience of a wall.

However, none of us has any way of ever knowing what the other person's experience of such dualities actually feels like to them. We have no way of knowing how light and dark actually appear through another person's eyes. We have no way of knowing how hard and soft actually feel to another persons touch. We simply agree to co-create and share such dualities so that we have a framework within which we can share the experience of our human world together. However, we are entirely free to experience those dualities in our own unique way. To share our human world together, we only need agree that such dualities exist.

If you find it hard to imagine that everything you experience in your human life might be your own unique creation, and that your experience of reality might be so different from anyone else's, then consider the world through the experience of an entirely different organism.

There are thought to be 1.5 billion times as many ants on our planet as there are humans, with a biomass around 25 times greater than that of mankind. Whilst there are estimated to be as many as 22,000 species of ant in our world, and mankind is a single species, many ant species do show a lot of similarities to humans. For example, ants are capable of building highly diverse social organisations. They have also been shown to communicate together and solve complex problems.

Ants are able to build massive colonies, some of which cover hundreds and occasionally thousands of kilometres. Such super colonies can be populated by billions of individuals, working co-operatively together. Some species of ant demonstrate the ability to grow and harvest other organisms as foodstuff, whilst others protect and care for different species from which they are able to extract nourishment in a sustainable way.

However, with relatively simple compound eyes, ants have poor to mediocre eyesight compared to our own. Ants also lack sophisticated ears to hear sounds in the way that we do. Instead ants build their lesser, ant reality using sophisticated antennae, which are able to detect chemicals, touch and vibration.

Whilst ants are undoubtedly self aware and arguably as, or more, successful than ourselves, they have achieved their success through experiencing a lesser reality that is vastly different to our own. How different would our world appear if we chose to experience it through the self awareness of an ant? Or for that matter, through the self awareness of any of the other species that we share our life experience with?

Given that there are so many species perfectly capable of thriving in our world, even though they construct their lesser realities in a fundamentally different way from ourselves. Why do we imagine that each of us must experience our own lesser, human reality in *exactly* the same way for us to be able to share experiences in our human world together?

3 WORKING IT OUT

In this chapter we look at how the ideas we discussed in Chapters 1 and 2, shape our everyday life. We explore how they might help us deal more positively with some of those aspects of being human that challenge us most.

Meaning and purpose

At some stage, most of us start to question whether our life has any meaning or purpose. For some, this question might feel like a chronic illness, nagging away in the background, year on year. For others, it might be far more acute. Coming to a head when we suffer most and then going away, once that suffering subsides.

There are many candidates for meaning and purpose. For those in poorly developed countries, the basic purpose of life can be as simple as attempting to keep regular access to food, clean water and shelter. Others are more privileged, and take such things for granted, perhaps believing their purpose to be the accumulation of material goods, or less tangible things such as giving free reign to their creativity.

If we were to generalise, some good candidates for an overriding life purpose might be; to serve, to care, to love, to suffer, to grow, to learn, to know ourself, to know God, to have fun or to experience pleasure. Indeed, all of these things can, on occasion, bring a sense of meaning and purpose into our life.

Some beliefs might try to persuade us that our life should have a single overriding purpose, and that without achieving that purpose our life will have no meaning. Sometimes we choose to adopt this view, to make things simple for ourself. However, as we travel through life, those things which once seemed so meaningful often fade away, and soon become forgotten. This is because meaning and purpose are not a constant or a 'one size fits all' commodity.

For example, when we are young, starting to create a world of our own, we might be materially driven. We might want a well paid job that enables us to have a comfortable home. At this stage then, we have chosen a life purpose that is about material acquisition. So the acquisition of material goods brings meaning to our life. Once we are established, we might want to have our own family, so we seek a mate. Our life purpose then becomes about nurturing offspring and the opportunity to become a parent, brings meaning to our life.

Later we might have experienced many ups and downs, and we might want to make sense of them all. So now, our purpose becomes the acquisition of wisdom, and a growing sense of wisdom brings meaning to our life.

Meaning and purpose are not absolutes, in our human world. They are simply that which we choose them to be at the time. We do not need to search for or understand meaning and purpose, to find peace and happiness in our life. Meaning and purpose are simply a reflection of those experiences that our self awareness is currently choosing to prioritise.

For our highest self, the concept of meaning and purpose is irrelevant. Our highest self knows that our human self is no more, or less than, a tool. A tool which the Something More uses to create an experience of itself, within that aspect of itself, that we know as our human world. Like any other tool, our highest self knows that the purpose of

48

our human self is to simply experience that which it has been perfectly designed to experience. In our case, to experience a unique human life as it passes through a shared human world.

We can imagine then, that our highest self might delight in any and every thing that we experience during our life. It might delight in the massive diversity of experience that we each choose for ourself, regardless of whether those experiences contain an over-riding sense of meaning and purpose or not.

Our highest self knows that we are simply here because we choose to experience being here. It knows that we need no greater meaning or purpose. It knows that all there is for us to do is to keep on experiencing whatever we choose, for the sheer delight of being able to do so. What could possibly be more wondrous than being able to create the experience of an entire human life of our own? With all it's thoughts, sensations, feelings, emotions, hopes, dreams and joys? What could be more magical than exploring the magnificent diversity of the Something More in human form? What could be more exciting than working with other aspects of the Something More to choose endless new experiences together, in a shared human world?

What greater meaning and purpose could our human self seek than being one of the countless eyes and ears of God?

Attachment and identity

As we journey through our life, we attach to many things. Our first attachments are formed with parents or primary carers; the people we are dependent on to provide the sustenance, safety, emotional support and guidance we need in our early years.

49

Then, as we start to find our way, we attach to other people and things. Our peers, partners, beliefs, interests, home, possessions, money and so on. Sometimes we attach to things that we might judge positively. Perhaps we find a friend who is very kind and helps us move forward with our life. We feel bonded and loyal to them. Sometimes we attach to things that we judge negatively. An abusive relationship that reminds us of a parent. A controlling manager that reminds us of an ex-partner. Regardless of whether we judge our attachments to be positive or negative, they take up a large amount of our time and attention.

We use our attachments to define ourself and shape our identity. For example; if I attach to a spouse, I see myself as a wife or husband. If I attach to a child, I see myself as a parent. If I attach to my work I see myself as a school teacher, nurse, doctor, businessman or whatever my employment is. We might imagine then, that our attachments serve us well, when we judge them to be positive, because they help us shape an identity within which we might choose to feel safe and secure. This is not the case.

As children, we attach to our carers because we are entirely dependent upon them for survival. However, as we grow up, most of us are capable of looking after ourself. But, we still become dependent upon those things and people that we attach to. This is because we fear that without them, we might have no identity at all. If I am not spouse, parent, friend, worker or any other of the things that I have attached to, then what am I?

Unfortunately, we know that all things shall pass. Our relationships will end by death or dispute, our children will grow up and leave us and our jobs will come to an end. So we know that all those things that we believe make us the person we are, are transient. At any time they might escape us and we will be left feeling less than we were before.

It is very easy for us to become trapped in a vicious cycle: The more we allow our attachments to define our identity, the more we fear we might lose them. The more we fear we might lose our attachments and the identity that goes with them, the more tightly we hold on to them. This is why many of us hold on to our attachments far longer than they continue to serve us. Because our fear of losing them and having open space ahead, seems far worse than putting up with the drudgery of something that we have already become numb to anyway. Holding on in this way can be a source of great suffering.

Our attachments also build walls around that which we believe ourself to be, and that which we believe we can become. For example; if I see myself as a painter of portraits, then I am less likely to explore the delights of painting abstracts. If I see myself as a composer of classical music, then I am less likely to explore the delights of playing jazz. Constrained in this way, I will not meet any of the new people, or have any of the new experiences that wait for me along those potential new pathways.

The more tightly we allow our attachments to define our identity, the more limited our concept of self becomes. The more limited our concept of self becomes, the more we restrict the life experiences that we are open to. And the more we restrict the life experiences that we are open to, the more trapped we start to feel inside. Again, this can be a cause of great suffering for us.

The challenges that attachment and identity bring us don't stop there. When we define our identity by specific categories, such as parent, wife, schoolteacher and so on, we automatically adopt a set of expectations about how we should and should not run our life. More often than not, such expectations are not our own; they are based on pre-conceptions we have chosen to inherit from others. Again causing us to feel trapped and unhappy.

From the perspective of our highest self, the suffering that our attachments bring, is completely unnecessary. Our highest self knows that we have no need to attach to people and things, in ways that constrain our identity or scope. It knows that people and things come into our life as we choose to experience them. Equally, it knows that as we have experiences in the human world, those experiences grow, transform, and come to an end. To our highest self, the fact that all things must come to an end, is not a reason to suffer. It is simply a part of the process that creates space for us to go on and choose to experience new things.

Sometimes things might end quickly, sometimes they might last a lifetime. In our human world, we have no way of knowing. However, as we deepen our self awareness, we see that we are so much more than anything that can be defined by the people and things we experience. Being so much more, we realise that we do not need to hold on to those people or things. They will be there as long as they will and they will end when they are done. Freeing ourselves from attachment, we can enjoy all that we experience, for what it truly is, in the moment. Then we are free to let it go gracefully, when the time comes.

Authenticity and aloneness

As children we are dependent on our parents for survival, so we allow them to start shaping our identity from an early age. As we become adult, it is therefore natural for us to turn to others; our peers, the media or authorities, to help us determine how we should act, and who we should appear to be 'out there' in the human world.

In truth, those that we have looked to for affirmation and direction, have probably been more engaged in dealing with their own life experience, than helping us to become all that we truly are. Unless we had particularly enlightened parents, very few of us will have been given unsullied guidance on what it is to be true to ourself. Very few of us will have experienced the freedom to develop naturally from birth into anything close to our authentic self.

More likely our parents will have unwittingly tried to pass their own fears and prejudices on to us. Many of us have been conditioned to be restrained, to fear change and to seek boundaries within which to exist. Our parents will have done this with best intention, telling themselves that they are fulfilling their responsibility to look after us, as vulnerable new people, coming into a dangerous new world. Most likely they were treated in a very similar way themselves, when they were children.

With so much to feel uncertain about in our human world, it is quite natural for us to seek acceptance, comfort and reassurance from others. Particularly because so much of what we choose to experience in our life is focussed on family, clan and kinship. However, your life journey is your own, and no one else can experience it for you.

In choosing to be a part of the human world, our self awareness has chosen to take responsibility for everything that we experience in our human life. That life is truly unique, and regardless of what we choose to experience, it is as worthy and meaningful as any other. No one else will ever experience the same life as you. So no one else is in a position to tell you how best to live your life.

It is not beholden on any of us to seek approval from others, or from the society we live in. We are all entirely free to make our own choices at any time (including the choice to need affirmation). We do not need to comply with, or take instruction from others, any more than it serves us in the moment.

As we will see, our highest self knows how deeply all of us are connected below the surface. However, it also knows that our self awareness must experience our human life as separate from all others, if it is to have complete freedom to choose whatever experiences it wishes. Each day, we must therefore stand alone with canvas and paint to create the unique picture of our life, and once that day's picture is complete it is ours and ours alone to treasure.

Different people deal with their aloneness in different ways. Some might choose large amounts of space, to ground themselves, connect to the world and regenerate peacefully in private. Others might choose a wealth of social interaction to energise and invigorate themselves. Most of us choose a mix of the two, in different amounts, on different occasions.

One of the challenges we face when we choose social interaction as a way to deal with our aloneness, is that it becomes very easy for us to fall back into the trap of believing that we need the affirmation and approval of others to be worthy of our human life. We lose ourself in what we imagine to be the opinions of others. Of course, although they might act to the contrary, those others that we depend on for approval, might be struggling to ground themselves too. We might find it hard to believe, but those whose affirmation and approval we seek most, to help us us deal with our aloneness, might be equally needy of our affirmation and approval, to deal with their own aloneness. Fuelled by anxiety, many of us have experienced such relationships, defined by power struggles, conditionality and insecurity.

If we choose a life where we believe we must rely on others for affirmation, then we entrap ourself in the human world and take ourself far from lasting peace and happiness. However, such complexities are not necessary. We are what we choose to be and at our core we will always be able to return to the authentic self that we were born to be.

Our **authentic self** is the expression of our highest self as it appears within the confines and limitations of our human reality.

We are authentic in those moments when we think and act in ways that are entirely true to our current understanding of self. As we are authentic in those moments when we act in ways that are entirely transparent to others. This does not mean that when we are authentic we shine with the true light of the Something More in the same way that our highest self does. For that is something which lies beyond most of us, most of the time. However, it does mean that when we are authentic we experience our life in a way that aligns us with our highest self and the many gifts that it can bring, allowing for the complexities of our human life at the time.

A simple way to imagine the relationship between the Something More, our highest self and our **authentic self** is to imagine a cloudy day. Above the clouds the sky is always blue and the sun shines on regardless. That is the Something More. Where there is a break in the clouds, rays of light shine through. That break in the clouds is our highest self. Where the rays of light strike a pathway, a road, a building or any other object, that is our authentic self.

If we move to stand in the rays of light that strike our world, we feel warmer, we become uplifted. From here we are able to lift our gaze, look through the gap in the clouds and delight in the clear blue sky and radiant sun that lie beyond.

In the same way, as we start to understand and live our authenticity our self awareness moves into the light that shines through our highest self. Our life becomes warmer, it feels safer, we become happier and more peaceful. We are able to lift our gaze. We are able to sense our highest self and the spectacular abundance that lies beyond.

When we live in authenticity, life reconfigures around us. We have a sense of becoming bigger, less bounded. We feel no need to be anything other than true. We understand the limitations of our human self and become kinder to ourselves. In the same way, we have no need to treat others with anything other than acceptance, caring and respect.

Developing our authenticity we come to understand that there is no place for anything other than positive intent in our life. With a life immersed in positive intent we find that the challenges and stresses that have haunted us for so many years, gently pass away. Not because we have 'gone out and fixed them' but because we have simply let them go.

From here, it soon becomes apparent that the limiting factor, defining the richness and depth of our life, has never been a hostile, constraining world. It has always been the limitations that we have unknowingly imposed on our own concept of self and the way that we have allowed those limitations to put boundaries around our choices in the human world.

From the perspective of our authentic self, we can at last start to understand our place in the universe. We realise that we no longer need material possessions, or power over others to feel safe, because we are so much more than those things. We do not need to own, control or compromise, because we need nothing more than to simply be ourself.

Connectedness

We might rejoice in the fact that each of us chooses a unique mind, a unique body and a unique life, different to any other. We might delight in sharing and exploring the variety and abundance of differences between us. Unfortunately however, our body and mind can be so preoccupied with the anxieties of survival, that we often see the differences between us as a potential threat. If you look similar to me, if we have the same language, beliefs and values, then I might feel that we are alike and that you mean me no more harm than I mean you. However, if there are material differences between us, then you are foreign to me, and my biology being what it is, tells me that you might be dangerous.

So when we are entrapped in our human world, many of us are afraid to express who we truly are, and what we truly believe. We are afraid to share our real journey with others in case we appear different to them and they reject us.

However, as we free our self awareness our perception of individuality changes. We come to know that, as wonderful as the differences between each of us might be, in the scheme of things they really are very superficial. Increasingly we see that our separateness is something confined within our everyday life. We see that what we appear to experience as separateness runs no deeper than the form of our body and the day to day workings of our mind.

If we know ourself to be no more than the body and mind that make up our human self, then we experience that body as a physical entity separate from, and unable to combine with any other, by natural means. And we experience that mind as something which, although able to exchange ideas and fleeting moments of intimacy, ultimately feels separate and alone from all others.

However, as we come to know ourself as both a human and a highest self, then we come to know our deep connection with all people regardless of race, colour, creed or disposition. We understand that as self awareness is simply that aspect of awareness which chooses to experience our unique human life, and as awareness is simply that aspect of the Something More which contains and connects all possible things, then below the surface, we are all comprised of the same stuff. We are all tied to, and formed of awareness flowing through and creating substance within the Something More.

In this way, we come to understand that we are entirely bonded, with everyone else in our human world. We understand that, below the surface, there is, ever has been, and ever will be, only one of us. In the same way that self awareness is simply one of countless facets of awareness, below the surface we are each simply one of the countless faces of our combined 'one self'.

From this perspective of deep connection we feel less a stranger in the world, we lose our fear of rejection and become confident to show our unique individuality. We start to delight in the differences between us and we cannot help but see others with a much deeper sense of understanding. Our compassion grows and as we start to find peace within ourself, so we find peace with others.

By understanding the depth of our connection we understand why those times when we voluntarily come together with others to exchange ideas, share a passion, or work on a joint project, can be so fulfilling. Because at those times we realise that our greatest human experience lies in our ability to co-create, at one with others, for the good of all.

With a concept of self so much greater than our human form, it is only a short step to realise that our connections within and beyond our human world are not purely confined to one another. They extend to all things. In the same way that you and I are simply different faces of one self, bonded by awareness, yet separated by our choice to experience a different life. Everything that we experience in our human world is simply an aspect of the Something More, bonded by awareness but separated by the choice to experience its own unique physical form.

The idea that all life might be interconnected is not new. Science has shown us for many years how elaborate our food chains and ecosystems are and how tightly we are bound together in the web of life. As we will see later, through our impact on the environment we have only just started to understand how many species are codependent on one another for survival.

Desires and requirements

In Chapter 1 we saw how, entrapped in our human world, it is very easy for us to feel anxious and uncertain. How many of us fill our life with distractions in the hope that we might worry less and feel more secure. We saw how using our life experiences and possessions to distract ourselves in this way we are constantly dealing with the symptoms, and never the cause of our worries. No matter how many things we do, and how many material goods we accumulate, we are never free from the insecurities and uncertainties of our human world, and as a result, our life can become overwhelmed with the constant desire for more. Our constant desire for more travel, more friends, more money, more possessions, more love, more power and the massive efforts that we make to gain such things, can have huge impact on the quality of life that we experience.

In addition, as we will see in Chapter 6, there are far more significant issues with respect to the rampant consumerism, that such desire based living creates in our shared human world. Such that at some point soon, we need to change.

If we wish to support our growing global population in the future, we will need to let go of our endless desires and come to understand that our world can only support us if we take no more than that which we truly need. We will need to move on from choosing a life filled with *desire*, to choose one from which we take only as much as we genuinely *require*. From the perspective of our human self, letting go of our desires might seem unthinkable. From the perspective of our highest self, things are far more simple.

Our highest self knows that we must experience food, shelter, sleep and warmth for our body to survive. It also knows that there are many other things that bring meaning and happiness to our life, such as friends, family and self fulfilment. Equally, it knows that choosing to relentlessly pursue our material desires will only cause us to experience suffering. However, our highest self does not judge anything that our self awareness chooses to experience, and will not intervene in any of those choices. Because to intervene, would undermine the ability of our self awareness to choose freely, and so undermine the massive diversity of life experience which we can create for ourself.

Our highest self knows, that all those things we desire to hold, and do, are simply fleeting distractions, compared to the boundless wonder of simply 'being', immersed in the experience of each moment. It knows that there is as much joy in peacefully looking at the changing shapes of the clouds, as there ever will be in acquiring expensive objects. It knows that simple interactions with strangers can be rich with love, compared to the superficial interactions that our human self might choose to fill time and provide distraction.

This doesn't mean that we have to renounce all of our possessions or reject all of our acquaintances to create a fulfilling life. What it means is that as we free our self awareness to sit more closely with our highest self, our possessions and relationships no longer hold the same meaning or value to us.

In letting go of our desires, we no longer fear that we might lose the things we have accumulated. Because we know that we no longer need those things to distract us, and we no longer need them to help us feel safe. In the same way, as we lose our dependence on material goods, we liberate ourselves from the experience of money-stress that so many of us co-create in this world together.

By liberating ourselves from money-stress, we come to realise that the universe will undoubtedly provide that which we require. It might not provide each of us with a yacht, a mansion and a fleet of Lamborghini's. However it will provide enough, and what it provides will be sustainable.

If you imagine cupping your hands together, then the universe will provide as much as you require to fill them. Some of us might have big hands and require a little more, some of us might have small hands and require a little less. Regardless, the universe will fill our hands with as much as we need to continue our life experience.

Driven by our desires, we can try to force more into our hands, but they will only hold so much. When we try to take more, we always suffer the experience of losing something else. This is why sometimes, no matter how much of our time and energy we throw into the pursuit of money or material goods, we never seem able to hold on to any more. Other times we do increase our material wealth, but at the cost of things like trust, peace of mind and happiness.

Anything that we try to take in excess of that which we can hold goes to waste. It is lost at the cost of someone else going without.

Judges and victims

In our human world, our mind attempts to make sense of life and to write a story that helps us feel good about who we are. We sort the things that happen to us, the things we think, and the things we feel, into categories separated by a line. On one side of the line, we judge things to be good, because they serve us in ways we can recognise as useful or pleasurable. On the other side, we judge things to be bad, because they appear either unpleasant, or unable to serve us. We believe it makes sense to have a 'bad box' which contains all of those things that we judge negatively. Because, by knowing what is in the 'bad box', we can be on the look out, to avoid similar things happening to us again in the future.

However, our insecurity and uncertainty mean that we can be very hasty with our judgement, when we put things into the 'bad box'. We listen to rumour and gossip, we believe the things that our media and politicians tell us. Often we judge other people and situations negatively, even though we have little genuine information and even less direct experience. Unfortunately, once something is in the 'bad box', we are very reluctant to take it out again.

Compounding the situation, when we believe that our judgement has failed, because we continue to experience bad things in our life, it is easy for us to become even more judgemental. So many of us come to see ourselves as victims of an uncaring and unkind world. A world filled with bad people and bad situations that are just waiting for the opportunity to take advantage of us. We become trapped in judgement and victimhood.

However, as we come to understand that we are so much more than the events we choose to experience, we come to understand how, as we saw in Chapter 2, we create and co-create our life experience in complicit agreement with one another. There is therefore no need for us to choose a life filled with judgement, as there is no need for us to imagine ourselves as victims. We also become aware that more often than not, it is our own anticipation and negative feelings about a situation that exhaust and demoralise us, more than the situation itself.

Our highest self knows that when our self awareness sits with our human self, we imagine that events are happening 'to' us. And because of causality, we often feel that we have very little control over those events. But this does not matter, because our highest self knows that, beyond our human self, we are entirely masters of our own destiny. It knows that, as we saw in Chapter 2, our self awareness chooses to experience exactly those things which it wishes to experience in the moment. If the universe appears to conspire against us, then our highest self knows that experience is ultimately our own choice.

As we move closer to our highest self, we therefore free ourself from imagining that we are the judges and victims of a precarious life. Instead, we see ourselves as free agents, responsible for all that we have and ever will choose to experience.

The idea that we have such incredible freedom might feel intimidating. Throughout our life we have been told that we are bounded and that our power is very limited. We have co-created a fearful human world that constantly tells us that we must be constrained and we must comply, otherwise we might become isolated and vulnerable. So why would we choose to stand apart and take ownership for choosing *all* of the things that happen in our life?

Why would we take ownership of the hurtful behaviour of *other* people towards *us*? Why would we take ownership for our failures, our disappointments, our unkindness, our greed and our selfishness? And if we did admit to ourself that we are responsible for such things, then wouldn't we feel somehow hopeless? Wouldn't we imagine ourself to be incapable of creating a tolerable life, and unworthy of the respect or support of our peers? At the end of the day, isn't it just easier to follow the pack and blame others for what we imagine to be our own misfortune?

If we choose to follow the pack and sacrifice responsibility in this way, we completely disempower ourselves. However, if we choose to take ownership, we grant ourselves a far greater level of acceptance and understanding.

This doesn't necessarily mean that by accepting responsibility we come to understand the chains of cause and effect that led to our current life experience. Nor does it mean that we become so adept at handling duality, that we can manipulate the world around us to avoid future unpleasantness. It simply means that deep inside we accept that anything we experience is ultimately our own choice. And that anyone who might challenge us is doing so because, at a deeper level, that is the experience that we have both agreed to co-create together. Because that is the experience that serves both of us best.

Growing in this way, we might see that each page we have written in the story of our life, has been filled with everything that we truly chose to experience in the moment. That when we wanted to experience happiness, we wrote its story in exactly the way that suited us best.

When we wanted sadness, we did the same. As we have done with fear, anger, jealousy and every other human emotion that we have chosen to experience so far.

Understanding the events of our life in this way we see how each of us has chosen to live an imperfect life as an imperfect being. That it is our imperfections that make us unique, and enable us to experience our own unique journey. We see that if we had wished to be perfect or have a perfect life, then we would not have chosen to be a part of our human world together. We know that it is no longer our place to judge, or attempt to change others. It is simply our place to accept and understand, as best we can, how at some level, their and our actions come to truly serve the both of us.

Pain and suffering

We have seen how self awareness chooses to experience everything it can of a human life, to the full. And how that choice means that it will immerse itself in things that our human mind and body find unpleasant, as well as things that they find pleasurable. We have also seen how duality determines that, in our human world, we cannot experience happiness without sadness, joy without misery and pleasure without pain. Pain and suffering are therefore an inevitable part of our everyday life.

In the same way that we might become trapped in judgement or victimhood, so we might become trapped in pain and suffering. For example, we might have woven a personal story in which we experienced hurtful things as a child. We might have chosen to take those things on as a part of our identity and, as an adult, keep reliving them again and again in different ways. Either because we are not yet ready to let them go, or because we are not aware of what we are doing. Unfortunately, the fact that we might simply be trapped in pain and suffering does not mean that they feel any less real or intense.

Because our feelings of physical pain can have survival value, they can be so compelling that they take over all of our immediate experience. Other times our life might be so deeply immersed in mental anguish that we are blind to anything else. However, as intense as such feelings might be, living in a state of suffering is ultimately a choice that we make like any other, and we do not need to become stuck with that choice if it no longer serves us. Just like being constrained by societal expectations, or over-attachment, being trapped in pain and suffering constrains the magnificent diversity of life experience that we can choose for ourself.

Our ability to find lasting peace and happiness does not depend on whether or not we experience pain and suffering, because at a human level such things are inevitable. Instead, our peace and happiness depend on how we choose to experience our relationship with the pain and suffering that we do experience. Equally, because our relationship with our pain and suffering does not require anyone else to co-create it with us, we are free to change that relationship whenever we choose.

If we choose to experience our pain and suffering as bad things, that bring us fear, cause us to hide behind walls and re-affirm our belief in a hostile, dangerous world, then our human life experience is diminished. However, if we accept that our pain and suffering are experiences that our self awareness has chosen, because it chooses to experience the full breadth and depth of everything that our unique human life can offer, then we accept that our pain and suffering are ultimately something that we welcome into our life. And they no longer become such an obstacle in our search for more lasting peace.

As we change our relationship with pain and suffering, so we come to understand that although there are some who experience a human life immersed in suffering that appears far beyond their control, many more of us choose to create our own pain and suffering from our fears, our judgements, our attachments, our resistance to change, our desire to control others and our inability to let go and let be. We see how we have chosen to hold on to all of those things so that we can build the boundaries around our life that we hope will make us feel safe and secure. However our life will not be constrained in this way, and in trying to maintain such boundaries we become exhausted. We are left feeling disempowered and vulnerable.

Very often we co-create our pain and suffering with others. So by changing our relationship with pain and suffering, we also change our relationship with those involved in helping us create it.

If we use our pain and suffering as a reason to justify our belief that we are surrounded by people who are dangerous, unpredictable and more powerful than we are, then we remain judgemental, victimised and constrained. However, if we accept that pain and suffering are our own choice, and understand that those who help us experience it do so in complicit agreement with ourself, then we no longer need bare animosity towards them.

By coming to understand how we invite others to play their part in our pain and suffering, we come to understand how the judgements that we made of other people and situations in the past were often a mirror, to reflect the personal boundaries which constrained us most at the time. We see that, because we chose not to look into that mirror at the time, and move on within ourself, we have gone on to choose pain and suffering in order that we might look again, a little harder. We realise that those who played their part in our greatest suffering were often those who invited us to face and overcome, the greatest boundaries that we had unknowingly set for ourself. That those who we imagined to be our greatest persecutors were so often our greatest allies and liberators.

This view might be hard to accept, if you are suffering right now. However, if we sit in our human world, immersed in our suffering and imagine that life is so unfair and so unkind; if we believe that we are the victims of people or situations that we judge to be so bad, and negative forces that are so much greater than ourself, then what hope do we give ourself of ever changing our life experience? If we lose ourself to our pain and suffering, how do we imagine we can do anything to experience a happier, more peaceful life in the future?

If, however, we allow ourself to accept that, yes, circumstances might feel very uncomfortable right now, but our self awareness has chosen, and agreed with all parties involved, for us to play our part in the situation. Then we allow ourself to explore the reasons that we might have made such a choice, and decided to be a part of such an agreement. We empower ourself to choose differently, as and when that situation has run its course and all parties are ready to move on.

When we take responsibility for our experiences of pain and suffering, we gain a better understanding of the likely outcome of things we might choose to do in the future. For example, we might see how by choosing a thoughtless, indulgent life experience in the past, that benefited no one other than ourself, we have invited duality to create other, miserable life experiences for us now, at the hands of others. Or, we might see how something that has recently hurt us, was the likely causal outcome of thoughtless events we initiated previously and had entirely forgotten about.

Likewise, if we cause pain and suffering to others, we can understand that we do this in complicit agreement with them too.

This doesn't mean that it serves any of us to create a life experience filled with cruelty. A life where we spare no second thought for anyone else. Because in the very least we know that, below the surface, we are all intimately connected as one self anyway. So any harm that we do to others we ultimately do to ourself. There are also other negative implications if we choose to cause harm to others.

For example, we might motivate them to kick off a harmful chain of cause and effect, with the intention of passing suffering back to us. Or we might perpetuate our own negative identity as someone 'bad' and 'unworthy'. On a wider scale, if we are hurtful to others, we continue to contribute to the co-creation of a fearful world view that undermines the lasting peace and happiness of so many.

The fact that we do create pain and suffering in complicit agreement with others, does however mean that we can revisit our relationship with guilt.

Guilt

As we experience suffering in others, many of us also experience guilt. Guilt can be the voice of our highest self whispering to us. It can be the voice that tells us the experiences we choose right now, might not fully serve ourself or others. Perhaps we are moving away from our authentic self, or perhaps we need to create new experiences that will enable us to start co-creating with different people. In this way, guilt can be very useful. However, many of us feel much more guilt than we need.

In much the same way that we might choose to become trapped in judgement, victimhood, pain or suffering, we might also become trapped in guilt. Perhaps we chose to be led there by resentful parents. Or perhaps we have chosen to take on ownership for traumatic events that occurred during our early life, such as our parents divorcing or abusing us. Although such experiences were probably way beyond our influence at the time, they may have caused so much suffering to ourselves and others, that we decided whatever happened was somehow our own fault. Hooked on guilt, we might choose to experience it at every available opportunity. Guilt closes around us, makes us anxious about new experiences and restricts our freedom.

Certainly, if we have just ploughed headlong into events that we knew might have destructive outcomes for others, then it can serve us to listen to our guilt. However, accepting guilt for things which we have not consciously chosen to participate in, or influence, does not serve ourself or anyone else.

As we experience the suffering of others, we know that, like us, they have chosen to experience a unique life in the human world. And like us, they have chosen to experience everything that life can bring, to the full. We also know that to be a part of our human world they have chosen to be bound by the agreement of duality that we all share. So we know that they too have chosen to experience both sides of pleasure and pain in their own unique way. The suffering of others is not therefore ours to own.

There is massive disparity in the material standard of living that we experience across our world, and most of us believe that this disparity creates suffering for many. However, as we have seen we cannot measure the life experience of another by our own. In the same way that our self awareness chooses to experience the diversity of our own unique life to the full, awareness also chooses to contain a global experience of all things, which is as diverse as possible. And we all sign up to play our unique part in that diversity.

As we experience suffering in others, we are free to offer help and support in any way we choose. We are free to engage in any causes that resonate with us. However, that does not mean we know what is right for those we offer to help. Nor are we in a position to judge the life that they choose to experience, as any better or worse than our own. We cannot measure the unique choices that another might make by our own standards.

Because guilt can have such a powerful influence on so many of us, we co-create a world in which we are constantly exposed to images and stories that use guilt to raise money or drive political gain. In our human world, guilt has become a weapon of power.

If we choose to take on guilt at the hands of others. If we choose to co-create a reality in which we let our humanitarian causes 'guilt' us into making donations, and our politicians use guilt to manipulate power, then we are left feeling conflicted and confused. Anxious about what we should, shouldn't, can and don't do. It is then a very short step back to the uncertainties and insecurities that cause us to co-create such massive dualities of wealth and power in the first place.

However, if we become more authentic and allow our self awareness to sit more closely with our highest self, guilt becomes unnecessary, it slips away from our life experience. Our highest self knows what serves us and others best. It understands our relationships and agreements with one another; how our life's journeys fit together, and how they are separate. Our highest self accepts the balance between the happiness and sadness

71

that we create for ourself and for others. Because it knows and accepts that is what our self awareness chooses to experience.

As it meets pain and suffering in the world, our highest self knows no greater joy than creating love, compassion and caring, unconditionally, for all. It knows the freedom of being able to give such things without attachment. Then gently let them go, without judgement, ownership, fear or guilt.

Taking responsibility

Entrapped in our human world, our need to feel safe, and our belief that there is safety in numbers, mean that, in addition to those boundaries which we set for ourself, we are often happy to accept boundaries that others might wish to impose on us. Unfortunately, such boundaries are usually imposed on us by others because they too feel insecure, and hope that by creating rules for us to follow, they might find more power, safety or security in their own life.

With so many boundaries and distractions it is all too easy for us to become trapped in a golden cage. We become institutionalised, happy to absolve ourself of responsibility for things which seem either too big or too difficult to handle. All too soon, we abdicate responsibility for our life's journey and simply do what we are told or do the things which we feel 'must' do.

Sitting in our golden cage, it can be extraordinarily intimidating to imagine that we have complete creative freedom to experience anything we choose. We might be overwhelmed by the idea of taking personal responsibility for a life of free choice. A life in which we knowingly take responsibility for all of the outcomes that we create, regardless of whether we choose to experience those outcomes as positive or negative for ourself, and positive or negative for others. Like the canary that refuses to leave it's cage through an open door, it might seem safer to simply carry on doing what we believe is expected of us, and blame others when we are not happy with the outcome.

However, if we are willing to take full responsibility for everything we experience, then we empower ourself to break free of our golden cage. We start to become authentic and we take a step closer to finding true peace, happiness and fulfilment in our life.

Taking responsibly means that we accept how deeply our life experience, and the experience of others, is effected by duality. So that we can take personal responsibility for how the dualities which arise from our behaviour, impact on ourself and others. It means that we understand how causality leads from one thing to the next, so that we can take personal responsibility for how our actions might lead to outcomes which harm others. And it means that we take responsibility for the difference between our desires and our requirements, so that we can avoid the negative impact that indulging or desires might have on others.

As we become more authentic, so it becomes more natural to accept such responsibilities. We come to understand that our responsibility extends beyond those things that we create and experience in our own life. Each of us is also personally responsible for how the things that we co-create together have impact on the world in which we live. When we take personal responsibility for co-creation in this way we start to realise how many of us co-create unconsciously, with little or no regard for collective outcomes. And we see how, on a global scale such behaviour can lead to life experiences that cause vast numbers of people to suffer.

For example, each day we meet wonderful, kind people. People that we can pass the time of day with and who bear us no animosity. If we need assistance then someone will usually come along to help us. Most likely from the kindness of their heart and expecting nothing in return. So for most of us, our immediate experience of other people is seldom anything but positive. However, for all the reasons we have seen, we know that vast numbers of us continue to carry fear, uncertainty and doubt within. Scaling these innate insecurities up to a global scale, we therefore co-create a global human experience that is filled with conflict, greed and xenophobia. Entire populations are displaced, religious groups are persecuted, and vast tracts of humanity are left without food, water or shelter.

As we come closer to our highest self, we understand that such issues are the inevitable outcome of our own fearful co-creation. We cannot hide and point the finger of blame at others. Such atrocities are something that we all own, because they are something that we all co-create together. Like the duality of money and poverty and the duality of powerful and powerless. These things do not stop until *all* of us take personal responsibility for letting go of the fears, doubts and insecurities that caused us to co-create them together in the first place.

Living with uncertainty

We have seen how, in choosing to participate in the human world, our self awareness has chosen to experience as much richness and diversity as possible. We cannot have a rich, diverse human life, unless we constantly choose new experiences for ourself. And we cannot have new experiences until we move on from old ones. So our life will, by necessity, be a journey of constant change.

We have also seen how on a far larger scale, awareness chooses to contain as much diversity and abundance as possible. Not only is our own life therefore in a constant state of flux, so too are all things that exist in the world around us.

Even if we didn't choose to experience constant change, we would still be subject to it, because our agreements of duality and causality mean that everything we create, creates something new. We swim in a constant river of change, regardless of whether we choose to go out into the world and 'make things happen' or whether we choose to stay momentarily still.

Change is not just a component of our life, it *is* our life. We do not choose a life which is subject to change. Our life is the *experience* of change. Duality and causality are not the agreements that cause change to happen, they are our agreement to experience change together.

Whilst we are at the centre of exactly the life experience that our self awareness chooses, we often feel that we cannot control or predict the changes that come into our life. This is in part because, at our current state of evolution, we are not masters of duality or causality. Most of us, most of the time, are so immersed in the experiences and imaginings of our human self that we seldom stop to consider the implications of our actions any more than one step ahead.

We also struggle to control or predict change in our life because our self awareness does not choose to have complete control over all that it experiences. During our waking life, our self awareness chooses to be part of a greater, co-created human experience and as part of this experience, it is immersed in a vast ocean of change, much of which it chooses to do no more than simply participate in. Immersed in so much change, we know that everything ahead is uncertain.

From the perspective of our human self such constant uncertainty can cause much anxiety. Our minds are masters at imagining future scenarios in which those things we most fear destroy those things that we hold most dear. So many of us resist change with a vengeance. We exhaust ourselves trying to hold on to things that we know we must lose, and trying to control things that we know are really way beyond our influence. Our anxiety about change can lead us to judge others negatively and dismiss people and situations that we feel uncertain about.

However, as we turn to face our highest self our relationship with uncertainty transforms. Our highest self welcomes uncertainty with joy. It knows that nothing new happens until we make space for it. It therefore invites open space ahead.

Our highest self knows that our human self often resist new experiences; fearfully telling us 'better the devil we know.' It also knows that if we overcome our uncertainty, let go, and allow ourself to move freely into the unknown, then we free ourself to break the repetitive and often destructive patterns of behaviour that cause our life to be so much less fulfilling than we sense it might be.

Our highest self understands how our life is underpinned by change. It knows that our self awareness does not choose a life that is pre-determined, with no surprises. It does not choose to be a passive participant on a guided tour. Our highest self knows that our self awareness chooses to be an adventurer and explorer, constantly creating its journey into uncertainty. It also knows that because we choose to do this, as a part of, and in complicit agreement with all around us, there is nothing to fear.

As we face our highest self we therefore understand how uncertainty brings us freedom. How uncertainty enables us to experience a life rich with choice and how, without uncertainty, our life would be so much less fulfilling. We see that if we choose to fear new experiences and try to re-form them into something more familiar, then we simply stand still, and exhaust ourselves fighting against the flow of our life.

We come to understand how, in the past, we have only chosen to make changes somewhere in the 'safe zone'. Somewhere between those things which terrify us, because they are our greatest opportunity, and those things which bore us, because deep inside we know they are really causal dead ends. We come to understand how such choices limit the depth and richness of our life and leave us feeling unfulfilled.

In accepting that life is nothing but the creation and experience of change, we realise that uncertainty is our greatest opportunity. Embracing uncertainty we are free to flow joyfully through the constant flux of our life. Free to immerse ourself fully, with open heart and loving intent, into the experience of each and every moment.

4 EVERYDAY LIFE

In this chapter we look at how, many of us, already experience the ideas and agreements we have discussed, as we go about our everyday life.

Natural metaphor

In Chapter 2 we saw how our experience of a shared human world is underpinned by our agreements of duality and causality. We then went on to see how, in coming to understand these agreements, we can start to make greater sense of our life, and the experiences that we co-create together.

Whilst duality and causality are the core agreements that allow us to share our human world with others, there are many other patterns and principles that influence our waking experience. Things like 'universal provision' explained earlier, and others like the 'impact of intentionality', the 'law of attraction' and it's duality; 'opposites attract'. These ideas have all been explored by others, in some depth.

As we develop a deeper connection with ourselves, we discover another principle that runs through our daily life. We discover that, if we make space to observe the world around us, then it shows us the things we need to make sense of our current life experience. We are surrounded by natural metaphor.

This doesn't mean that the natural world chooses to teach us, as a parent might teach a child. There is no college degree we must take to become qualified in natural metaphor. It is simply the case that, as all things are ultimately connected, all things ultimately exist in unity and in harmony, and all things therefore reflect one another.

Because awareness contains and connects the experiences that our self awareness chooses to make a part of our human life. None of our experiences exist in isolation, they exist as a part of an entirely connected whole. So as we pass through each day, like the ripples from a pebble dropped into a pond, the things we observe in the field of awareness around us, shape and form, to reflect the essence of that which we currently choose to experience. This principal underlies oracular practices such as the I Ching.

For some, such ideas might seem far fetched. However, many of us regularly experience how the world around us appears to reflect the world within us. For example, we might notice that on days when we feel positive and enthusiastic, then the people that we meet seem upbeat, happy to share pleasant interactions with us. But on our sad days, other people also seem depressed, remote and disconnected. We can choose to see such synchronous experiences as simply the fact that people we meet are intuitive and so, being sensitive to our moods, tend to mirror our behaviour. Or we can choose to see them as an indication of some deeper underlying connection and resonance. As with so much else, what we believe is purely a matter of choice.

Natural metaphor is not complex and it can speak to us in very personal ways. For example, we might be struggling to deal with a personal issue and observe an ant trying to move a large object on its own. That ant may be joined by a colleague and together they might succeed in their task. From this it is easy to imagine that natural metaphor is showing us the reason we are stuck is because we need help from somebody else. On another occasion we might feel that life is dealing us so many challenges we simply cannot cope. In which case we might go for a walk on a windy day and observe how branches which bend in the wind stay intact, whilst those that are rigid and brittle, break off. Perhaps now natural metaphor is showing us that it is time to be more flexible, bend and accommodate the situation.

The fact that natural metaphor is so deeply understood by all of us, means that it is widely reflected in our use of language. Each day we might face a 'mountain we have to climb'. We might fail and 'sink in quicksand'. We might come to realise that we were always 'walking on thin ice', so decide to 'turn over a new leaf' and 'branch out'. Or perhaps we might decide it is time to 'come down to earth' and 'put down roots'. Having left 'no stone unturned' we might then go through a period of 'playing cat and mouse' and eventually decide it is better after all to settle for 'a bird in the hand'.

All of these phrases describe ideas that are far more complex than the few short words they contain, and illustrate our intuitive connection with nature. Natural metaphor resonates so deeply with most of us, that often the best way to communicate a new or abstract idea is to relate it to something common, that we all have prior experience of in the natural world.

If we create enough space to experience it, natural metaphor can be a magnificent gift. It not only provides us with a constant source of guidance, it also helps us feel our true connection with everything around.

Natural metaphor shows us how each moment of our waking life is not just something we experience alone. Instead, that moment is an aspect of the single, unified, creative experience that flows through all things. Natural metaphor shows us how, below the surface, no strand of that unified experience can ever exist in isolation and how all things and the experience of them, are bound as one.

Knowing ourselves to be a part of the whole, in this way, we can see the world with fresh eyes. We can allow ourselves to wonder at the magnificent creation in which we choose to participate. We can see that, rather than the vulnerable, isolated human entities that we once imagined ourself to be, we are completely at one, connected and in dialogue with each other, and with all that surrounds us. We flow as one, together with all that has, does, and ever will, exist.

Dreams

We don't know why we need to dream. However, we do know that if we don't dream our mind and body are unable to function normally. Dreaming is an essential part of our human life and at times our dreams can be as intense and compelling as any experience we have when we are awake.

The content and purpose of our dreams is not definitively understood. However, over the past 100 years there has been much research into dreams and their meaning. With eminent psychiatrists like Jung proposing that dreams are a way of communicating with something deep inside, below the level of everyday consciousness.

For thousands of years, people have used their dreams as a way to gain insight into waking life. Cultures such as the Australian Aboriginals believe in a 'Dreamtime' realm beyond space and time; a realm that they believe we can enter through our dreams, transcendence or death.

For some, dreams can have very personal meaning and their interpretation can bring a far deeper sense of self, as well as a better understanding of current life events. As a result, there are numerous psychological and mystical traditions that have attempted to define a language of dreams for us.

For others dreams might appear obscure and worthy of little attention. However, even those who don't see the relevance of focussing on their dreams, can be moved to reflect on their current circumstances by a memorable dream or nightmare experience.

Undoubtedly, some of our dreams do relate to our waking life. However this is not the full story, and as we start to develop a greater understanding of self we can start to look at our dreams in a slightly different way.

One of the things that our dreams show us, is that self awareness is entirely capable of experiencing convincing realities at will, and involving all of the senses, without the need for input from any external or shared human reality. Not only do our dreams show us this, they show us that we need the space to create such unconstrained realities for ourself. Otherwise we cease to function in the waking version of reality that we choose to co-create in our shared human world together.

As we have seen, we choose to co-create a shared human world in our waking reality, because it vastly increases the diversity of experience available to us. This means that during our waking reality we are bound to the agreements of duality and causality. In our dreaming realities however, we are not bound to those agreements. This is why, in our dreams, things can jump from one experience to another, in no clear sequence, and things can happen with no apparent outcome or implication.

Our dreams reveal the depth of our creative power and how important it is for us to have freedom to experience that power to the full. They show us how central we are in whatever reality we choose to experience.

Most of us imagine our life to be comprised of a waking reality, which is real, interspersed by periods of sleep, which we have to have, but don't really understand why. However, if we change our perspective a little, we can see that our life is really comprised of *all* that our self awareness chooses to experience whether we are awake or asleep. Certainly it is comprised of a bounded, waking reality played out in a human world. However, it is also comprised of multiple, unconstrained, dreaming realities. Perhaps our self awareness chooses to experience such unconstrained dreaming realities as 'down time' to slip back towards the Something More. Or perhaps as time to grant itself full creative freedom; time to delight in it's own unique creativity entirely free from constraint by others.

Perhaps then the only real difference between our waking reality and our dreaming realities is the fact that we choose to co-create our waking reality with others. Whilst we choose to create our dreaming realities alone.

There is a subtle linkage between the structured, co-created human reality of our waking life and the free flowing, unconstrained reality of our dreams. In the same way that natural metaphor might guide us through the events of our everyday life. Our dreams might help us understand why we choose some of the experiences that we do.

If we listen openly to the language and metaphor of our dreams, they help us become more authentic and take a step closer to our highest self. If we choose to listen, our dreams show us how each and every one of us sits at the creative heart of our own world. And how each and every one of us is therefore entirely free to choose whatever life experience we truly wish.

Love

Love might be one of the most widely misunderstood words in the English language. For most of us, 'love' is a universal 'catch all' that describes any manner of things which bring us pleasure. We make love, we love our parents, we love our children, we love our friends, we love our pets, we love watching a movie, we love listening to music, we love dancing, we love singing, we love painting, we love playing sport, we love walking in the rain, we even love eating ice-cream, the list goes on.

Our experience of love can be many things to many people. It can be intimate, erotic, committed, fatuous, romantic, infatuated, passionate, consummate, trivial or empty. Our shops abound with symbols of love, social media is filled with sayings about love, and endless self help guides encourage us to connect more deeply to the love within and between us.

We understand love in so many different ways. When one person uses the word love, another might give it an entirely different meaning. Yet we place so much store on those four simple letters. We search for someone that we can fall in love with; someone we believe will bring us the things we cannot find within ourself. We fail to stay in love with them because deep inside we realise that the things we seek, to make us whole, are our own responsibility and no one else's. We choose a life partner because we love them or are in love with them. We choose a parent for our children on the same basis. We build families, to share our love, then we disassemble them, because we have fallen out of love or because we are in love with someone else. Yet if any one of us was pressed to articulate exactly why we allow love to drive our key life experiences in this way, most of us would probably struggle to come up with a convincing answer.

Whilst many of us idealise our love to be something kind and freely given, in the human world, the opposite can be true. Many of us negotiate love and it's various manifestations to gain the things we desire, such as material security, sexual favour, or emotional power. Using love to serve ourself in this way can be very subtle. Often we don't even admit such behaviours to ourself. But for so many of us, in the human world, our love can be both conditional and highly selective. It is often something that we use to help us deal with the insecurities and uncertainties of our physical existence. In the human world then our love, however we define it, is very often tied to need.

As we become more authentic, so our perspective of love changes. We come to understand, that which we genuinely experience in our life as love, is simply our direct experience of the Something More running through our human world. From the perspective of our highest self, the distinctions that we make between the various types and categories of love are entirely irrelevant, other than providing diversity and variety to our life experience.

Our highest self knows that, regardless of the experiences that we choose to share between ourselves, and regardless of how we choose to judge those experiences, we are unified and animated by the true love that flows between all people and all things. At this level there is no difference between the quality or quantity of love that we share with anyone, or anything. We understand that our love is genuinely unconditional. It flows freely between ourself and others, regardless of the role that those others might play in our everyday life.

From this perspective we see that, as with change, true love is not just a component of our life experience. It *is* our life experience. True love is not something which comes and goes between us dependent on circumstance, desire or need. It is an unconditional, non-exclusive, eternal absolute.

Whether we choose to experience true love in our human life or not, it is the very essence of the Something More that flows through our thoughts and feelings. It is the core of awareness that animates our human self and unites us with everything else. Whilst, in our human world, we might choose to experience vast differences in our feelings towards those we agree to like, dislike, love and hate. In truth, true love pervades all and accepts all, equally.

Our highest self knows that, like change, love 'just is'. It knows that we are united by the true love that flows in equal measure between every single one of us. It knows that the love we feel for strangers, for enemies and for all we experience, is no different from the love we might feel for our friends, our children, our closest partner or for ourself.

Peak experience

We have seen how, no matter what life experiences we choose, the vast majority of us imagine ourselves to be bound by the thoughts of our mind, the actions of our body and the constraints of our human world. This is perfectly normal, and as it shall be. However, most of us have at least one story to tell about experiencing something which we cannot explain from the perspective of our everyday life.

Some might have experienced a sense of time slowing down, or personal boundaries dissolving, in quiet moments of contemplation, or in those frantic split seconds before an accident. Others might have experienced shared dreams or a deep sense of empathy and connection with people they are attached to and places that move them.

At some stage in our life, most of us actively search for the sense of freedom and expansion that comes from experiences outside our everyday reality. We seek moments of release and union through sexual intimacy. We lose ourself to the rhythm and harmony of music. We have even created a plethora of narcotic drugs to consume, in our quest to be more than our everyday human self.

Many of us might also have had experiences of 'flow'. Flow can come to us through deeply co-ordinated physical activity, such as dance or sport. Equally, for those who enjoy creative activity, it can manifest as a sense of connection to some higher creative force. Most who experience flow find it deeply rewarding. Through it they discover the joy of existing, all be it temporarily, in a state which lies beyond the confines of their human self.

Our experiences of something greater are not purely confined to recreational activities. Many of our most famous scientists and inventors document that their eureka moments did not come from conscious thought. But instead, arose quickly and spontaneously within them, as if coming from the deep subconscious or some higher intelligence.

At the other end of the scale, some of us choose a life devoted to the quest for transcendent experience, which we imagine might change our relationship with the human world.

Transcendent experience can arise spontaneously; perhaps associated with physically or mentally traumatic events. For example, surviving a traffic accident, or experiencing childbirth. However most who seek transcendence, do so either through a journey focussed primarily on mind, such as meditation, a journey with a stronger emphasis on the body, such as yoga, or through religious devotion.

As mentioned in Chapter 1 our language is built around words and concepts that describe life in our everyday human world. The things that we choose to experience in transcendence however, are not of that everyday world. So, there are no words to adequately describe such experiences. The simplicity of a moments transcendent realisation might take a lifetime of human description to explain.

In moments of transcendence we don't *understand* what it is to exist outside of time, we *experience* the eternal now. We don't *understand* what it is to be a single facet of an entirely connected whole. We *experience* what it is to be unbounded, dispersed through all things. We don't *understand* how awareness passes synchronously between us. We *experience* what it is to flow in harmony with all. Equally, in transcendence we come to know that such experiences, as profound as they might be, are simply another facet of awareness, beyond which lie infinitely more that we have no capacity to experience, let alone describe or discuss.

Whatever transcendence experience truly is, it is extraordinary. Such experiences can be overwhelming and have no reference point in everyday life. When we allow our self awareness to shake loose from the entrapment of mind and body, we are fundamentally changed.

As we return from transcendence we might imagine that we have gone somewhere. Perhaps to some other dimension, place or time. This is not the case. Throughout our life experience we remain with body and with mind, even if our self awareness chooses not to experience them. During transcendence however, our self awareness moves a little, it loosens it's attachment with the body and mind and settles in a place closer to the flow of awareness. A place where our human reality of time and space are no longer required. A place beyond the confines of duality and causality.

Our transcendent experiences are not separate from our day to day life. They are simply moments when our self awareness 'tunes in' to a different level of being. In the same way that we might choose to tune in to a different T.V. or radio channel. Of course all of those different T.V. and radio channels are being broadcast all of the time. But we only have the equipment to receive a limited number of them, and we can only tune in to any one of them at any one moment in time.

Through the course of our life most of us choose to stick with the channel we know best, because we have no idea what other channels might be out there. So it is with the many states of being that we might experience through the course of our life. They are all out there, we just don't choose to tune in to them.

Our transcendent experiences are no more or less real than any other of our day to day experiences. They do not take us anywhere else and when we tune back into normal life, that life goes on as normal. However, such experiences can have a profound effect on our concept of self and our choice of life experiences going forward. Through moments of transcendence we loosen our attachment to self, to others and to the ego. We start to lose our fear and anxiety. We know what it is to be truly calm and at peace with ourself.

Transcendent experience brings us a greater sense of connection and compassion. Through it, our life can start to make more sense, our values, priorities and perspectives can start to reshuffle. At the level of body, transcendent experience might help us develop a sense of physical well being. Our senses might become heightened. Our dietary preferences might change, drawing us away from substances that we imagine have harmful effects on our body.

Such changes can be overwhelming, particularly if we have experiences of transcendence that arise spontaneously, without following any particular mental, physical or spiritual discipline. However, studies indicate that these profound initial experiences settle over time, to a constant sense of calm, connection, peace, happiness and well being.

As magnificent as transcendent experience can be, it does not need to be a specific goal for any of us, and we do not need to experience it, to experience our human life to the full. The peace, happiness and fulfilment that so many of us seek, are not an outcome of anything that we do. They are not an outcome of anything that we have. Nor are they an outcome of anything that we experience. They are an outcome of that which we imagine ourselves to be. And whether we encounter transcendent experience or not, each of us is free to imagine ourself to be anything we choose, as and when we are ready.

5 PULLING THINGS TOGETHER

In Chapter 5 we draw together the themes and ideas from Chapters 1 to 4 and look at some of the first steps each of us might take, on our journey towards a more fulfilling life. In the appendices, there are more practical ideas about different approaches we can take and the things we might find along the way.

Trust and surrender

As we have seen, many of us believe that our whole life is bound to a reality made of material objects in an entirely physical universe. A reality in which, no matter how wealthy or powerful we become, we will soon pass away and amount to nothing. It is understandable then, that we attempt to fill our life with distraction, rather than face the deep uncertainty and vulnerability that we know lie within.

In this book, we have started to question some of the discrepancies between that materialistic world view and the subjective experience that makes up our own personal journey. Instead of accepting a purely physical reality, we have come up with a different way of seeing things. We have explored the reasons why the human reality that most of us choose to believe in is so compelling. And how choosing to live in a purely human world binds us to our mind and body, in such a way that we cannot avoid being driven to create life experiences rich in anxiety and insecurity.

Of course our new model of reality is no more or less real than any other. It is simply a tool that we can use to help enrich our life, or lay aside for future reference.

Having a tool that enables our mind to work beyond the limitations of our physical world does make a lot of sense. It makes sense of the challenges that we face within ourself, and it makes sense of the world that we choose to experience together.

More than this, it shows us that we have the freedom to become completely true to ourself. And that the self we find when we do become true, might be so much more than we had previously imagined. Our model invites us to let go of our fears and become all that we can be. Together, it enables us to create a world so much greater than the vulnerable planet that our relentless consumerism and material appetites continue to devour.

In our model we are no longer small, vulnerable organisms subject to the whims of a mighty universe. We are the creative centre of our individual and collective human experience. And each of us is entirely empowered to choose whatever human experience we wish for ourself.

Our model shows us how we bring diversity and richness into our life by becoming co-creators of a collective reality, in equal agreement with others. It shows us how, as entities far greater than body and mind, we are deeply connected to, and form a part of, all that exists around us.

Our model helps us understand why our lives unfold in the way they do and why no two lives will ever be the same. It goes on to explain why we agree to share experiences that we judge to be both good and bad. In part, because we have agreed that our shared human reality cannot have one without the other. Also, because in choosing to experience a human life, we choose to experience everything that life can bring. The full range of feelings and sensations, the good and the bad of it all.

Our model allows us to put aside the negative judgements that we so often make of ourself and others. It shows us that we always make the right choices, based on our current interpretation of a situation, and on our higher agreements with one another. Knowing this, we cannot escape the conclusion that right now, in the moment, everything is as we have chosen it to be. Although each of us has chosen to be imperfect, the totality of all exists, and will always exist, in a state of perfection.

Our model shows us that lasting peace and happiness are not things that we obtain through consuming life experiences or material goods. They are not something which becomes ours by following a self-help program, getting a new job, a new partner, or a new life. Lasting peace and happiness are not things that we have to hold on to in the world around us. For the world around us will always be in a state of uncertainty and change.

Certainly, if we use our mind to understand how our experiences are shaped by duality, causality and co-creation then we can bring more peace and happiness into our everyday life. And that is very worthwhile. However, like everything else in our human world, the peace and happiness that we do bring into our human life, shall pass.

Lasting peace and happiness are things that flow constantly through and within us. So to find them, we must look beyond our physical and mental form. If we believe we are genuinely ready to live a life which contains more lasting peace and happiness, then we can only live that life from a place outside the confines of our human world and deep within ourself.

For all the reasons we have seen, we can not create lasting peace and happiness for ourself, if our concept of self is no greater than the limits of our body and mind. So our model is about exploring that which lies beyond our body and mind. It is about developing our self awareness. About coming to accept that the human world we feel bound to, is only a very small part of something altogether more magnificent. It is about each of us knowing that, as we stand alone at the creative heart of our life experience, we are bonded with all who choose to share that life experience with us.

Our model is about accepting the limitations of our human self and having the courage to look beyond. When we do this, we might see ourself as flawed and inadequate. However, our flaws are the very things that we choose to make us unique. They are the very things that enable us to create our own unique life experience.

Our model shows us that each of us is perfect in our imperfection. That if we have the courage to take just one step closer to authenticity, then our life will start to transform. In authenticity we develop a sense of our highest self. We start to accept all that we are and grant ourself the space to grow.

We do not need to be yogi's or gurus to grow in this way. Nor do we need to adhere to any particular religion, spiritual belief or behavioural system. We can simply choose to create space to start discovering what we really are. Then we can choose to create life experiences that enable us to become what we have discovered. We can choose to let go of the person who is attached to the uncertainties, insecurities and expectations that constrain our everyday life. We can choose to turn and face the authentic self that we were born to be. It really is that simple.

If we can accept that there is so much more than we are able to touch, hold or measure, then we can accept that, we are something far more than the person we have chosen to become in our human world. We are something far beyond our true understanding or description.

It is a simply matter of trust.

Are we so afraid of the world we have created for ourself that we have to hold on tight and limit our life to that which we feel we can control? Or are we willing to let go, surrender and place our trust in something so much greater than our current concept of self?

Many live in faith and enjoy just such a journey of trust. They come from all walks of life, all cultures and all beliefs. So why would we not choose to join them? Why would we continue to hold on to the attachments, fears and insecurities that bind our life and make us miserable? Why would we face away from the beauty that lies within?

All that we experience in our human world, we will lose soon enough. Perhaps in the next breath. And we know that if we stay firmly entrapped in that human world, we are unable to overcome our biological anxieties. So what have we got to lose if we choose to experience our life differently? What is the worst that can happen if we accept that we might be more than just a mind and a body? What is the worst that can happen if we free ourself to explore what that more might be?

How bad will it really be if we choose to step beyond every single boundary that we have ever set for ourself?

If fear tells us that in stepping out we could lose everything, then how bad will it really be if we take just one small, gentle step at a time? If we start by crossing only those boundaries that don't really matter to us any more?

It is not the size of the steps we take, that helps us grow in self awareness. It is the fact that we find the freedom and courage, to keep moving forward. The fact that we find the freedom and courage to submit to the magnificent flow of our life. The freedom and courage to trust, surrender and knowingly immerse ourself in the river of uncertainty that defines every moment of our human experience.

True path

Because each of us chooses to be entirely unique, we each have our own unique way of travelling our life's journey. We therefore each have our own, unique 'true path'; a path that flows easily for us and along which we find it perfectly natural to be authentic. Our self awareness might choose a wide variety of experiences, so our true path can meander through life, heading in different directions at different times. However for many of us, at some stage, our true path might well lead towards greater wisdom, authenticity and the experience of our highest self.

We know we are on our true path when we are passionate about the things we do, when we care, and things really matter to us. We know we are on our true path because we spend hours absorbed in doing things that captivate us, we work late into the night, or wake up early. Not because we are anxious and unable to sleep, but because we have a brilliant idea that we are so excited about. Equally we know we are far from our true path when we experience apathy, indifference, fatigue, boredom and anxiety.

Unless we are 'called' from an early age, it can be very difficult to know where our true path lies. When we are young, for all the reasons we have already seen, we often feel great pressure to comply with what we believe others expect of us. We become immersed in the roller coaster of our life and soon lose sight of what we really care about.

Unfortunately, this makes us neither peaceful nor happy.

It can take great courage for us to step aside, stand alone and make space to consider what our life has become. However, by doing this we grant ourself the chance to re-discover who we are and what really matters to us. Once we have re-discovered what really matters to us, it can take even more courage for us to face our fears and realign our life with our true path. However, when we do this the rewards are immense.

It doesn't matter if our true path, right now, is to be a nurse, a teacher, an actor, a street cleaner or a scientist. It doesn't matter if our true path, is to be a parent, a carer, a leader or a follower.

Aligned with our true path we can not help but passionately throw our energy into all that we do. For we are in our chosen place, the place where we fit, the place where our experiences flow naturally and effortlessly. On our true path we work for the joy of it, we work because it enriches us and makes us feel complete. On our true path we have an innate understanding of the things we need to do, when we need to do them. We feel our greatest sense of purpose, we are happy and fulfilled. Our true path makes our life experience rich in a way that it never could be before.

On our true path we trust ourself and we trust the universe. We become authentic and transparent. We know that the more we throw our self into that which we are here to do, the less we need worry about all those insecurities that used to fill our life. We know that we are in a place where the universe will not only provide for us, it will align with us, and actively help us keep moving in the right direction.

On our true path, we know that we are free to let go and let be. We are free to simply get on with living our life to the full, and let the 'rest' look after itself.

First steps

If you knew that you would live this instant again and again through all eternity, then what would you do differently? What would you feel differently about? How would you re-prioritise the choices that define your life right now?

If you would change something, then why haven't you done so already?

Perhaps you imagine that you are constrained by someone else, someone who might not take kindly to you making more free and independent choices? Or perhaps you imagine that others have far less tolerance of your individuality, and desire for self expression, than they really do?

But have you ever tested these things? If you have tested them, and found that others really are trying to control you, then why do you choose to remain trapped?

It is understandable that we use other people as an excuse to avoid doing the things we are anxious about. Some of us don't have the confidence to feel comfortable making life decisions, and want to be told what to do. Some of us feel safer having boundaries set for us.

However, as we have seen, whilst others can share many wonderful gifts with us; helping us to experience love, kindness and virtue in our relationships, our life's journey is our own, and no one else's. Each of our pathways is intrinsically unique and no one else's to judge or control. If we seek greater self awareness, if we choose to become more authentic and wish to find greater fulfilment in our life, then that is something that we must do for ourself, something we must do in our own unique way.

Certainly there are many faiths, beliefs, practices and techniques that might help broaden our self understanding. As you start to take your own steps forward, you might explore many fascinating ideas. You might find one particular path that resonates with you. However, no one else can tell you how best to live your life or what best serves you in the moment. That is your choice and your choice alone.

All that you require is available to you, all is possible, and all can have value.

It is up to you to shape and continually re-shape your life, in the way that you choose. It is up to you to explore and take on those things that best serve you, for as long as they serve you best. When those things cease to serve you, then it is up to you to have the courage to leave them gently behind, move on, and explore new things.

This doesn't mean that you should not commit to anyone or anything. Nor does it mean that it serves any of us to choose whatever we want, whenever we want it, regardless of the impact on others.

It simply means that your journey towards greater self awareness is a journey of self. A journey of coming to know your self, and coming to *be* your self, at a fundamentally deeper and more connected level. As you connect more deeply and come to experience more lasting peace and happiness within your self, so do you create more lasting peace and happiness for those who share your world with you.

There will be many steps on your journey to self. Appendix 1 contains a few simple ideas about approaches you might choose, to keep your life moving forward. A good starting point might be to question your strongly held beliefs, how many of those beliefs are really your own? How many of them have you taken on from your parents, peers or culture? How many perpetuate your anxieties and hold you back? How many empower you to think and act freely?

You might also choose to put time and energy into exploring new ideas, with an open heart and open mind. What do other people believe? How do they choose to live their life? How do you feel about their beliefs and choices? Do they resonate with you in a way that you want to explore? Or do they feel cold and empty?

One of the most striking things we discover as we embark on our journey towards self, is how simple life really is. How little of what we previously imagined to be important, really matters. We see how many of the distractions that used to occupy our life were never really relevant to the experience of living.

Growing in this way, it soon becomes apparent that, throughout our life, we have put massive efforts into perpetuating those dramas that we claimed caused us to suffer. We see how many of those things that we said we wanted to stop, we actually continued to re-create, without realising. Perhaps because we knew no better. Perhaps because we felt the need to comply with others. Or perhaps, because, with the relentless noise of fear, uncertainty and self doubt numbing most of our waking hours, we simply needed to create drama, to feel fully alive. When we come to see our journey in this way we understand why our life was so exhausting. Why we so often felt trapped, bored, unfulfilled, or just numb.

The move away from a demanding and sometimes overwhelmingly complex world, filled with fears, desires, thoughts, strategies and actions, can be disorientating. So Appendix 2 looks at some of the issues that we might encounter as we continue on our way.

One thing that we do encounter as we move forward is the sense that what we have now, and what we are now, is enough. This brings us inner stillness and in our stillness we discover open stretches of silent inner landscape.

At first, that silent inner landscape might feel unfamiliar, we might become uncertain. True to our biological nature, we might search for new things to worry about. But creating new worries no longer serves us. Instead, we can choose to become familiar with inner stillness. For it is in stillness that we feel the true peace that has always flowed within us. It is in stillness that we can hear the soft whisper of our highest self.

It is in stillness that we can at last create our own truly unique life, free from constraint, free from fear, at peace with ourself and magnificent in all that we have chosen to become.

6 34 DAYS

In this chapter we look at why it is so important for each of us to develop a deeper sense of self at this pivotal stage in the evolution of our species. The issues covered here are very broad and will be dealt with in far more depth in the future. They are raised here to illustrate how important it is for each of us to take responsibility for our own self development, if we wish to ensure a future for our children and for generations to come.

Taking stock

In the early pages of this book, we saw how mankind has chosen to evolve at an unprecedented rate. How we choose to live in a complex digital age, yet remain entrapped in our basic, cave person bodies. We saw how one of the reasons we have evolved so quickly, is because we have a unique mind. A mind which enables us to work constructively together to experience so much more than that which we could experience alone.

One of our greatest challenges however, is that, although our minds help us to co-operate together, both our mind and our body remain programmed for survival, in what we imagine to be a fundamentally hostile world. Even more challenging, is the fact that many continue to believe that their survival is nothing more than the continued existence of their physical body and those of their immediate kin. Such a limited view of self may contribute to the downfall of our species, or it might be our greatest opportunity.

Right now, we co-create a human world that we appear unable to sustain.

Across the globe, there are approximately 1 billion of us experiencing lives in 'well developed' countries. Countries which have a good supply of resources, food and water. There are another 6 to 7 billion of us experiencing lives in 'less developed' countries where the supply of food, water and material goods is less predictable. Whilst the population of well developed countries is expected to stay relatively stable, the population of our less developed countries is expected to reach around 8 billion by 2050.

Over the past 40 years, those of us who have chosen to experience a materialistic life, based in a well developed country, have had a massive impact on our world's natural resources. At our current rate of consumption, it is predicted that our oil supplies will last another 35 to 50 years, our natural gas will last 40 to 160 years and our coal supplies will last 250 to 400 years. These fuels bring us the energy we need to keep ourselves warm, to keep cool, to cook our food, to travel and to run industry. Right now, they make up 87% of our energy supply across the globe and we have no viable, scalable alternative. They also form the basis of many of our medicines, plastics, lubricants, cosmetics and synthetic fabrics. Without them, such things might cease to exist.

Many of the rare earth metals such as indium, platinum and silver, essential to the production of our technology, are projected to become so scarce within the next 10 to 20 years, that we will be unable to afford to use them in consumer products. We have been unable to identify substitutes for 12 of the 62 most scarce of these materials. So right now, the future for much of our consumer technology also looks uncertain. Even aluminium may become prohibitively expensive to extract over the next 80 years. Without aluminium we would struggle to produce aircraft and other forms of transportation that we take for granted. Again, right now, we have no substitute readily available.

Perhaps more worrying, is the impact that our choice to live materialistic lives, in well developed countries, has had on the rest of our natural world. Global warming has been debated for many years. However, the massive impact that our species has had on biodiversity is less widely publicised.

According to the United Nations, by 2010 intensive farming and the use of fertilisers had already caused soil biodiversity to reach 'very high' to 'extremely high' threat levels, across most of Northern Europe. In effect, leaving the land infertile, so we are unable to feed ourselves without adding large quantities of nutrients to the ground.

Unfortunately only 30-50% of the chemicals that we pour onto our fields are absorbed by crops. Much of the rest runs off to pollute our coastal waters where it has led to the creation of 'marine dead zones'. Marine dead zones are areas where the sea contains so little dissolved oxygen that it can no longer support most marine life. There are over 500 marine dead zones; stretching along the North American Coastline, much of the European Coastline, the Southern Coast of Japan and the South Western Coast of Australia . With around 80% of our fish stocks classified as 'fully exploited', 'over exploited' or 'depleted'. The richness of our oceans, like so much of our soil, is severely compromised.

Coupling these changes with our impact on the climate and global warming, we are choosing to create a planet that is under extreme pressure. Increased desertification, drought and the use of water for agriculture, places our water supply at risk. Whilst competition for the use of land by biofuels, and to house population growth, means that, in order to feed ourselves, we must destroy wider and wider tracts of the natural world.

The next 40 years look set to become the perfect storm for our species and for life on our planet. It is estimated that we are losing between 1,000 and 10,000 times more species per year than the natural, background extinction rate. With top end estimates of as many as 100,000 species becoming extinct every year, many ecologists warn us that we may already be in the midst of a global extinction event, equivalent to the demise of the dinosaurs.

The extinction of a species becomes news when it involves large predators, or marine mammals. However, it is no less impactful for our selves or our planet, when we lose species that we barely notice. For example, in the past 5 years the north american honey bee population has collapsed; with only 50% of hives surviving. Honey bees are essential for the pollination of our food crops. If honey bees were to become extinct, a vast range of the foodstuffs that we currently take for granted would no longer be available to us. So it is with all species, all are tied in the web of life together. And for all the reasons we have already seen, we are all co-dependent on one another in ways that are far beyond the ability of any of us to truly comprehend.

Much of the damage that we have done to our world can be largely attributed to the 13% or so of us who live in well developed, industrialised countries. Currently there are around 2.5 billion people living in China and India, both of which are countries that have not previously been considered well developed but whose economies have started to grow with the expansion of global trade and ample low cost labour.

At our current level of evolution, we have no reason to believe that the middle classes of such developing countries will choose to experience anything other than the materialistic lifestyles that those in our well developed countries have already chosen. Should this be the case, how long do we believe it will take us to create a planet that simply cannot sustain us any longer? How long do we believe it will take for us to lose the ability to create sufficient food, fuel and water for ourselves? And how do we believe we will respond, as a species, if and when such things happen?

So we are at a point of transition. The next two generations might represent our finest hour. The point at which we consciously evolve beyond our basic human fears and aggression. The point at which we choose to let go of the greed, materialism and secular beliefs that we cling to in the hope that they will help keep us safe. Or we might simply choose to carry on co-creating the chains of cause and effect that will lead to the demise of our species. Either way, the experiences that lie ahead are, as they have always been, our own choice.

We can turn to our religions to help us, certainly the belief that there is a higher authority or higher order can serve us well. It can bring us humility, a sense of equality, a sense of being more than just material. It can bring us a sense of wonder.

However, if our religions have developed a human power base which uses them to justify intolerance, inequality, bigotry, violence or narrow minded compliance, then they are unlikely to help us. And for the good of ourselves, and all who choose to share the experience of this planet with us, it may be time for us to leave them behind.

We might also choose to leave our religions behind if we use them to justify our abdication from personal responsibility. If we use them to deny that we are responsible for choosing everything that we experience in our life. And if we use them to deny that we are all responsible for co-creating everything that we experience in our shared world together.

We can turn to science and technology to help us. We have only just started to experience how international travel helps us share cultures face to face, and mix the gene pool to benefit our species. We have only just started to use digital communication to build virtual communities which transcend geographical, political and even legal boundaries. And we can only start to imagine how, through fusion, the production of unlimited, clean energy might entirely transform our life experience and choices, in the future.

If we do choose for our species to survive, science and technology may well be essential in helping us support a stable, higher density population across the globe. And in working out how to do so in a sustainable way. However, science and technology are unlikely to help us if we continue to invest their resources in developing consumer products that do little more than distract us from the uncertainties of everyday life. Equally, the use of science and technology to develop and maintain military equipment, so that our leaders may attempt to rule by force, is unlikely to assure the survival of our species. It is more likely to lead to our early demise.

Similarly, we are unlikely to create a human world that is sustainable, a world in which each of us is granted the basic necessities of survival, and a world which is more equitable for all, when we allow our political leaders to spend so much of their time negotiating the physical, economic, legal and religious boundaries that make up our feudal nation states. And when we allow them to spend so little of their time working out how to come together to share resources, talents and opportunities on a global scale.

2000 generations

Issues like global warming, species collapse, poverty, powerlessness, intolerance, corruption, greed and violence might seem way beyond any one of us to resolve.

However, if we truly choose for our species to survive, not just 2 generations, but another 2000 or more, then as we have seen, that choice starts with each and every one of us, it is not something that we can expect those with power or influence to do for us.

At our current state of evolution, many who choose to have power, are as immersed in the our collective fears as any of us. They exist within economic, religious and political governance structures that have grown from those collective fears. And as they have succeeded in fulfilling their own need for power or wealth, by working through those structures, there is no reason for us to expect them to do otherwise.

As our societies and systems become increasingly complex, those with authority attempt to implement ever increasing levels of command and control, in the hope that they might be able to retain influence for a little longer. However, governing our societies through increasingly complex laws, omnipresent surveillance, non-human systems and strict penalties creates a population who are fearful, conflicted and resentful. It also wastes massive amounts of energy and resources, on a global scale. It is not therefore a part of the solution, it is a part of the problem.

The only way that we will build the peaceful and productive societies that can assure our future, is by allowing ourselves to evolve into peaceful, productive individuals. The only way that we will take violence and terror out of our world is to take fear and insecurity out of ourselves. The only way for our species to survive is for each and every one of us to evolve into something that has survival value.

Our survival therefore depends on each of us evolving in such a way that our current systems of governance become obsolete. As soon as those systems start to become obsolete then collectively we will start to let them go. We will create space, and we will find alternatives that serve our species and our planet far better.

However, our current systems of governance will not become obsolete until we evolve beyond our basic instinct to be controlled by the fears and uncertainties that define our biological existence. They will not become obsolete if our greatest concept of self is our material wealth. And, if all we wish for ourselves and for our kin, is to build a life focussed on hoarding material goods or temporary power, regardless of the impact that such behaviour might have on others.

Our species will build a lasting future, when each of us chooses to grow in self awareness, when we know ourself to be so much more than the fears and insecurities that pervade our body and our mind. And when we know ourselves to be capable of so much more.

As we grow in self awareness we understand how deeply we are connected, how that which we do to others, we do to ourself. How the diversity and wonder that we choose to take out of our world, we take out of ourself.

In this way, as we grow in self awareness we cannot help but choose a greater future for our kind and for our planet. In making such a choice each of us can choose to accept that the time has come to change some of those things that we have resisted throughout the development our civilisations.

For example, we can choose to let go of the geographic, political, fiscal and religious boundaries that segregate us. We can can choose to let our population re-distribute and stabilise, at a density, and in a pattern, that is sustainable.

We can choose to become a single global community that delights in, rather than fights over, its own rich diversity.

If you are living comfortably in the developed world right now, then re-distribution of our population might seem unthinkable. However, we have seen how population increase and changing demographics threaten to have massive impact on *all* of us. No matter how much wealth or power we might try to hold on to, that impact is something that *none* of us can escape.

There are also other less selfish reasons why we might choose to tear down the boundaries between our nation states. With our population and resources distributed as they are, so many live in environments that will never be able to support them. Why would we expect those who see their children die of disease or malnutrition, simply cease to attempt to have more children? Why would we expect them to give up the right to experience what it is to be a parent? And how can we expect them to sacrifice the richness of their own life experience in this way, when in part, it is us who have chosen to create so much imbalance and disruption to our world in the first place?

Other than allowing our populations to re-distribute and stabilise then, what other humane choices do we have?

In re-distributing our population we begin to break down the geographical, political, fiscal and religious boundaries that perpetuate the inequalities and intolerances of our world. We therefore free ourselves to demilitarise. We free ourselves to strip out duplicate fiscal, legal and political administration. And we can remove the inefficiencies of international trade and exchange, so that we are free to distribute our global resources efficiently, effectively and equitably.

In this way, when we are ready, we can free ourselves to evolve beyond a monetary economy and strip the profit motive out of industry. We can re-focus science and technology on providing clean energy, sustainable food and water for all. And we can divert our efforts and resources back into repairing the damage that we have already done to our planet and to it's inhabitants.

Once more then, we are faced with personal choice. We can choose to take responsibility for ourselves and adapt to become a global species. Or we can choose to leap headlong into the abyss. In evolutionary terms we might have very little time left. However, as we saw in Chapter 1 the one thing that our species is spectacularly good at, is evolving *very* quickly.

At a personal level, we might decide that those things which happen two generations hence do not concern us. But is there any amongst us who can look into the eyes of a laughing child and truly say that they do not care whether that child lives or dies? Is there any amongst us who can experience the image of a starving infant, close to death, and not wish that we could create something better for our kind?

At a personal level, we might decide that the challenge is too great. On the face of it, it is. The world that we co-create together is so much greater than our individual concept of self. However that is not the point. The world that we co-create together is a *part* of *all* of our individual selves. It is a collective whole that *all* of us participates in creating together. The future that we co-create together is not something that we need see as inevitable, any more than it is something that we can 'hand off' to anyone else.

We change the future by changing ourselves. There is no other way. Each of us is the source of all that we experience in our individual and collective human life. So if we want to create our world differently then we must choose to create ourselves differently.

If we want to create a species defined by inequality, suffering and eventual collapse, then we can choose to create our life as something defined by fear, anxiety, anger, greed, materialism and selfishness. However, if we want to create a species that works together to ensure it's survival, to care for one another, and to delight in the diversity of all things, then we can choose to create a life defined by authenticity, peace, wonder and service.

In finding peace within ourself we are free to move on from those things that have caused us to behave so destructively towards one another and towards our planet, in the past. We are empowered to take our place in shaping a new future for our kind. Not because we imagine others expect it of us, we feel it is something that we 'should' do, or something that we are paid to do. But because we come to understand that shaping a future for our kind and for our planet is our highest calling. It is that which we truly choose to do for ourself. It is our highest expression of self, and we are no longer afraid to be all that we truly are.

Our choice to build a lasting future for our species lies in our choice to evolve beyond our basic human drives and urges. That is not to deny that those drives and urges exist. But to fulfil them responsibly, knowing ourself to be so much more.

Our future lies in our choice to mature and evolve beyond mindless consumers of a planet, that is running out of resources and resilience. To become adult custodians of a planet that we know to be a part of ourselves. And adult custodians of all that choose to share the experience of our planet home with us.

We will create some kind of future for our species. That future might be extinction. We might no longer choose to come to this life and experience what it is to be human, because that particular journey might be nearing it's end. We may choose to create population collapse, famine and disease so that others might choose to experience re-building a new world, with greater wisdom, once the cycle is complete. Or we may choose to take responsibility and nurture ourselves and our planet through this critical stage. Should we choose to do this, to let go of our fears, cross our personal boundaries and come together as one, then we choose more time for ourselves. And in time, the stars might truly be ours.

All is possible. All starts within. All starts with self. In coming to know our self more deeply, we come to understand that divinity is not something granted to historical characters, mystical beasts or people in authority. Divinity is something that flows through each of us, as it flows through the heart of all created things. Our personal relationship with the Divine reveals the strength and depth of our connection to the totality within which we exist. It brings us to the light. And illuminated we are free to share that light with all who we meet.

It could take us 34 days to share our light with every single human on our planet. 34 days to start a magnificent new journey together. 34 days to become adult custodians of the most magnificent creation that we might ever conceive or experience. We have forty years. That journey starts now, with each and every one of us.

APPENDIX 1: APPROACHES

Some of the ideas in this book might have helped you see yourself differently and start to make new choices in your life. Or they might help you feel more confident about the choices you have already made. If that is the case, then it has served its purpose. However, for those who want practical ideas about how to start or continue to make change in their life, the following pages outline some simple approaches that might help you keep moving forward on your journey towards greater self awareness.

Realism

We have seen how each of us chooses to create a unique life, rich in all that being human can offer. And that by default, by choosing a human life, we choose to experience things which we might judge to be unpleasant as well as things which we might judge to be pleasurable. So it is not realistic for us to expect to choose, or be capable of experiencing, a human life which is filled with activities and situations that bring us pleasure and happiness all of the time.

It is realistic however, for us to choose to deepen our understanding of duality, causality, co-creation and connection, so that we understand how such things shape our life. It is also realistic for us to choose to become more authentic. To choose to develop our self awareness, come closer to our highest self and experience moments when we are not so tightly bound to the constraints of our human life.

It is realistic for us to choose experiences that create deeper peace and happiness within ourself. And to come to accept, with calm equanimity, those experiences that previously caused us so much suffering. As it is realistic for us to choose to take full responsibility for the outcomes of our choices, not only on ourself, but on all who share life with us.

It is also realistic for us to take personal responsibility for the differences between our desires and requirements, so that we can start to build a sustainable life and repair the damage we have done to our planet over the past 40 years.

Questioning

We have seen how deeply our life choices can be influenced by what we believe others expect of us. Typically we express such choices, that are not our own, with words like; 'should', 'shouldn't', 'must' and 'mustn't'.

We have also seen how most of us have spent much of our life trying to conform with what we believe society expects from us. However, binding ourself to the expectations of others in this way, does not help us understand or become the unique individual that we were born to be. Nor does it help us deepen our self awareness and become more authentic. Instead, it keeps us entangled in the dramas that others choose to create in their own lives, and locked into the collective fears and anxieties that we choose to co-create so widely together.

As we develop our understanding of self, we might choose to question the assumptions and choices that we have made in the past. In particular, we might choose to question those choices that we feel uncomfortable with, on the inside. Those choices that bring us inner conflict because they take us further away from our authentic self.

An easy place to start might be to question our 'should's', 'shouldn't's', 'must's' and 'mustn't's'.

Through questioning, we become more honest with ourself about why we behave in the ways we do. We come to see and know ourself more deeply. We start to re-discover our authenticity, and the implications of our behaviour become more apparent. In this way we start to consider new choices that are less bound to the expectations of others, and more aligned with who we truly are.

Space

Whilst many of us gain moments of happy distraction through our social interactions with one another, for all the reasons we have seen, self awareness, authenticity, our experience of highest self and lasting peace and happiness, all flow deep within. They are not things that we can be given by others.

Admittedly, for those who choose a particular faith, spiritual discipline or self help program there can be great benefit from sharing ideas and experiences with others on a similar path. Having a guide, mentor and supporter can be very beneficial. However, our relationship with ourself is something that we live in private. So if we choose to deepen our relationship with self then ultimately we will need to find space to do so in solitude. We will need to find space to be completely free from the distractions that so many of us choose to fill our everyday life.

We cannot hear the gentle whisper of our highest self, when others are shouting in our ear. We cannot feel the gentle caress of the Something More when our bodies are being assailed by physical stimulation.

Making space means removing those things that no longer serve us from our everyday life. For example:

- Get rid of anything that you don't truly require. In particular recycle those things which have any form of ambiguous or negative connotation for you. This will help you become more confident about letting go of things that no longer serve you. It will also make space for new things to come into your life.

- If your journey has been materially abundant so you now have a larger home and/or more significant assets than you require, downsize and pass them on to people who really need them. This will help you let go of your materiality, serve the common good and bring you into a new environment, where you might be more open to experiencing new ideas.

- Only buy the things you truly require. There is no value in filling your life with clutter that does not serve you and there is no point in continuing to co-create the materialistic habit that causes so much damage to our planet.

- Let go and let be. Every day we encounter situations which require us to make decisions. If no decision is obvious right now, and right now it is not essential to make a decision, then let it go and let it be. This will free up mind space for you to experience other things that serve you better in the moment. It will help you stop ruminating about the past, engage in the now, and stop worrying about the future. It will also help improve your ability to live with uncertainty.

- Take fewer drugs. Nicotine, alcohol etc. We have seen how many of us use drugs as a primary form of distraction. This does not serve us, as it damages our body, takes our time, brings us money-stress and, in the moments when we are under the influence, can lead to us kicking off random, often destructive, chains of cause and effect. As we reduce our drug intake so we grant ourself more conscious space to create and experience things which serve us better.

- Get off grid. When you are ready to spend time alone, get away from other people. Know what it is to exist in solitude and isolation. Stop doing. Sit in silence and allow yourself to observe how different the experiences of your body and mind are when you have no distractions. De-focus and see where your thoughts run. Grant yourself time and space to find, accept and love that which you truly are.

Acceptance

No matter how much suffering we bring into our life, things are as they are. We always make the right choices based on our interpretation of a situation at the time, and on our higher agreements with one another. Others make their own best choices in the same way. And however those choices might affect us, we have already agreed, at a higher level, to be a part of them.

So it serves us to be at peace with the choices that we do make, and not to judge ourself negatively for making them. As it serves us to be at peace with the choices that others make, and not judge them negatively either.

If we want to make peace with ourself, then we can choose to accept that there is no one to blame. And we can choose to accept that it serves no one if we take blame or guilt on ourself.

If we want to experience more lasting peace and happiness in our life then we can accept that we choose the ups and downs of our life in the same way that we choose all of our life experiences. And we can accept that, by necessity, all things exist in a constant state of change and uncertainty. We cannot control other people and we cannot control most outcomes.

Courage

It takes great courage to accept that life may never feel perfect. To question the utility of those things that we have clung on to for so long, in the hope that they might bring meaning and value to our life. To question those things that others cling on to for identity and security.

It takes great courage to clear space in our life. To sit alone in silence and accept all that we truly are. Great courage to accept that we are entirely responsible for the choices and experiences that make up our life.

It takes courage to accept responsibility for all of our interactions with others and for our part in co-creating so many of the issues that we experience in our human world today. Courage to accept that there is no one to blame, not even ourself.

It takes courage to become authentic, to seek a true path and to follow that path. As it takes courage to welcome change, immerse ourself in uncertainty, let go and let be. Courage to recognise our fear as our friend, and as something that constantly reminds us how much greater our life experience can become.

However such courage is an intrinsic part of the unique human life that each of us has chosen to experience. It is not beyond any of us and, if we fear our next big step, then we can pause, take a rest and choose to take just one small step at a time.

Exploration

In the same way that it serves us to question the authenticity of our existing choices and beliefs, it also serves us to explore new ideas and experiences. There are so many things to explore. For example:

- **Nature**. We have seen how the natural world is in constant dialogue with us, and how deeply we are attuned to that conversation. As we make space in our life and let go of the pre-conceptions that stifle our awareness, we can delight in that dialogue and those magnificent things that it shows us.

- **Wonder**. The more open we become and the more space we create in our life, the more we can wonder at the diversity and complexity of our human experience. Certainly nature abounds with incredible textures, patterns, interactions and interdependencies. However, there is wonder in most everything we experience. From the diversity of global agriculture that ends up producing our evening meal, to the complex engineering that makes up the most simple car. Wonder abounds in everything, as we explore it, we cannot help but connect more deeply with ourself, and come to understand more fully, our place in the human world together.

- **Knowledge**. Our species has created a vast pool of ideas and information about every aspect of our world. Investigating science, technology, the arts and humanities can help us delight in, and value, the true diversity of our life experience. Whilst we have seen that we are unable to discover or even understand absolute truths, acquiring knowledge can help us understand our self, our world and our connections more deeply. It can greatly increase our sense of wonder.

- **Self Help, Spirituality and Religion**. There are a vast array of self help, spiritual and religious paths that can help us on our way. Many of them can guide us as we explore concepts greater than our everyday human life. They can help us find a way towards greater self understanding and greater self awareness. We are free to investigate any of these pathways for what they are. They are tools which we can choose to use for as long as they continue to serve us. Like everything else in our human world, the truths that they explore are relative, not absolute.

- **Creativity**. Everything that we do is creative. Everything that we have or have experienced in our life is something that we have created for ourself. Bringing our creativity into focus, through the arts, can be a fantastic way of exploring our inner self. If you are worried about the judgements that you believe others might make of your efforts, then you can explore your creativity in private. If you are worried about the judgements that you yourself might make of your efforts, then you can choose a form of creativity, in which you enjoy the process, rather than produce a tangible outcome.

- **Connection**. Do things for others, purely for the sake of it and expect nothing in return. Explore how it feels to give freely and unconditionally to others. Practice doing the same for yourself. Share your new ideas with others and see how they respond to you. Not for validation, but to see who is going to help you on your journey, and who is not. If people aren't going to help you, or continue to accept you, then you can choose to stand aside from them for now, all things will change. Associate with new people who are on their own journey of self discovery. Let go of people who are deeply entrapped in the drama of their material life. Explore the concept and experience of re-inventing your relationships with others as different faces of our one self. Try to see yourself through the eyes of others.

Kindness, passion, patience and ownership

It will serve you to be kind to yourself, to leave old wounds alone and let them fade. It will serve you to do the things you really care about. To let go of the things you don't really care about and don't really want to do.

It will serve you to do the things that you feel passionate about in the moment, and to learn patience if the situation determines that now is not the right time to do those things.

If something brings you peace and happiness then it will serve you to keep doing it for as long as it continues to do so.

It will serve you to keep reminding yourself, particularly when life challenges you, that all is choice. As it will serve you to accept responsibility for all that you experience in your life, the good, the bad, the happy and the sad of it.

When times are bad or sad it will serve you to ask yourself 'how does it serve me to experience this in my life right now'. And if the answer to that question is that it does not, then it will serve you to peacefully let it go.

APPENDIX 2: INTEGRATION

Some of us find it perfectly natural to experience a life free from the constraints and expectations that define our societies. However, many of us have always felt bounded by what we imagine others expect of us. For most then, our journey to self is an evolutionary process that does not begin until we are genuinely ready.

As we gain life experience we might start to realise our mortality and question what we wish to experience in whatever time we have left. Questioning ourself in this way, it can be quite natural to grow beyond the need for money and power, to mature and look more deeply into ourself.

Our journey to greater self awareness is the journey of a lifetime. There is no destination that we must reach, no end point. No two journeys are the same and as with all journeys, much of what we encounter along the way may be unexpected and inexplicable.

This Appendix draws on, and dives deeper into, some of the key themes covered in preceding chapters. It identifies a few of the way-marks that we might experience once we embark on our journey to self. Undoubtedly your journey will contain many others, which you discover for yourself.

Shifting relationships

As our self awareness grows, it is natural for us to feel differently about our current life and the people who choose to share that life with us.

We come to see that the closeness and love we feel for others; our partner, our children, our friends or our parents, are all magnificent gifts. But we know such things are destined to pass. We cannot escape the fact that the life experience we have chosen to co-create together is bounded. It has a beginning and it has an end. That beginning and that end are ours alone and we have no way to determine at which point any of us might choose to leave our human world behind. We lose friends, relatives and loved ones.

We also see that many of our close relationships might be fraught with challenges and are not always the reliable source of peace and happiness that we imagine they could be.

In coming to know ourself more deeply, we understand that we must turn inward for the sense of completion and fulfilment that we previously tried to find through others. For in the end, all that we will ever have is the singular life that we have chosen to experience within ourself. In the same way that we would not want, or be able to meet, the responsibility of providing for anyone else's peace and happiness, our own peace and happiness never were and never will be anyone else's responsibility.

In coming to truly understand our independence, we might start to feel isolated and alone. We might start to see our friendships differently and feel confused about how best to service our relationship with our family. This is a natural process. It is simply a reflection of the fact that we are choosing to change our inner reality and create a new perspective. We are choosing to embark on a slightly different journey, because we believe that journey will serve us better. And we believe, that by serving ourself better we will ultimately be able to serve others better.

Like any other new journey, at the start, we might encounter all sorts of experiences that we never expected. This process can be particularly challenging if we come from a background which is highly materialistic, structured or rules-bound. However, the experience of new and unexpected things is exactly the reason why we have chosen to create our new journey in the first place.

As we continue to move forward, it becomes easier to relax into the new, to flow more gently. Some of our relationships might be challenged, and it might be time to let them go. However, working through this period we allow ourself to build new relationships with different people. People who connect with us in different ways and bring new richness into our life. Likewise our relationships with those we continue to hold dear become more transparent, more consistent, and easier to understand.

Seeing the cycles

As we grow in self awareness, we might see that many of the challenges we have had so far, seem to keep happening again and again. Each time we experience them, they might take on a slightly different form, but in content they are exactly the same.

For example, one year we might embark on a new intimate relationship. We might put all of our time and energy into it, only to find that after a few months, our partner has moved on to fresh pastures, leaving us feeling empty and used. In the same way, the following year, we might feel that our friends are not loyal to us. Perhaps, despite the efforts we make to be kind, generous and considerate, they seem to keep taking us for granted, then moving on.

Previously, we might not have noticed such cycles, or the similarity between these two different situations. We might have just felt tired and demoralised by all the effort that we have to put into our life, to simply stand still. We might have judged others as bad and selfish or ourself as unable to choose an appropriate partner and friends. However, as we journey towards greater self awareness, we become one step removed from the ups and downs of everyday life. We become one step more aware of the patterns we are weaving.

Very often, as we identify a pattern or cycle we soon create the opportunity to experience it again. This is our chance to experiment with it and explore new ways in which we might choose to experience it differently. If we are not ready to break the cycle, or change the pattern, then we will experience it once more, perhaps changing it the next time. However, if the cycle has now fully served us, we will take the opportunity to approach things differently and finally move on. With no need to experience that particular cycle in our life any longer, it is unlikely to return.

Writing our book of eternity

One of the implications of a model of reality so much greater than our purely human world, is that everything we touch, see, hear, taste, smell, feel, imagine, experience and create is simply a component of something far greater. In our model, the Something More that contains our human life, is unbounded in both time and space. With no absolute dimension of time, the Something More therefore contains all things, and all possibilities, right now and forever. This means that everything that we have and ever will experience already exists throughout eternity.

Our human life is the flow of eternal instants that our self awareness chooses to experience in sequence. With each moment, our self awareness draws an experience from the infinite resources of all that has, can, or ever will be and writes it down as the next unique page in our personal book of eternity.

Knowing ourself and our life process in this way, it becomes quite natural for us to loosen our grasp on the constraints that we might previously have believed governed our life. With such a vast concept of our place in eternity, it becomes far easier to let go of our limiting human construct, to empty ourself and to allow our highest self to act through us.

At this level of self awareness, our life exists more often in a realm akin to flow. Only now it is not flow initiated by occasional physical or mental activity. It is the natural flow of the Divine operating through us. It is the flow of us becoming an open channel to the universe. The flow of the Something More that, as awareness, connects and unifies all created things. In this state of self awareness we understand how such flow is present at all times. How it is the very life force that animates our experience of body and mind.

When we feel such deep connection with ourself, with all around us and with something so much greater, we realise that the individual identity which so many of us cling on to is but a tiny facet of all that we truly are.

We realise that, as a part of something so much greater that ourself, all we can do is resign sovereign authority and give in to willing submission. We accept our place as a part of the whole, and understand that we have no more to do in this life than immerse ourself fully and freely in writing the next moment, whatever we may choose it to be, into our own personal book of eternity.

Dealing with disorientation

We have seen how, as we choose to experience a journey towards greater self awareness, many new things might come into our life, and many old things might start to appear differently. How, as our relationship with ourself starts to change, we might find that our relationships with others start to change, so we might become confused about our identity.

As we explore our human life in more depth, we might start to have unusual new experiences that we are not sure how to process. We might start to re-shape our physical and emotional world in ways that serve us better, or in ways that create the space for us to move on.

Our first experiences of becoming more a part of the whole, and less a part of our human self, can be very disorienting. Equally, the experience of then slipping back into everyday life can leave us wondering what is real and what is not. Some of the more profound experiences we might have, such as willing submission, resignation of sovereign authority and transcendence can be overwhelming. Particularly if we choose to grow in a rapid, spontaneous or unstructured way.

However, none of these experiences are things that we need to fight. They are simply a choice that our self awareness might make when the time is right. They are part of a natural process that enables us to understand the difference between our highest and human self. A process that shows us how the experience of our highest and human self *feels* so different. How we navigate our creative life experience differently in each state, and how we are free to choose different states of self awareness at different times.

As we choose to experience such changes in our life, so we can know that, even though those new experiences might feel disorienting, they are the things that serve us best in the moment. We need not fear them and we need not fear losing our way. We can come to understand that disorientation itself, is a choice that we make, to lend significance to our new experiences.

Most importantly, we can know that there are many in the world who share a journey similar, but not identical to our own. There are friends, supporters, guides and mentors waiting for us, and soon enough we will meet others who we too are able to help on their way.

Settling into everyday life

We have seen how, in choosing to be human, each of us has chosen to create an everyday life which is deeply immersed in the experiences of a human body and a human mind. How in choosing to be human we have chosen to play out our life with all of the earthly passion and energy available to us. And in choosing to be human we have chosen to write a story grounded in our co-created experience of a shared human world together. So we do not need to step outside of our human body, our human mind or our shared human world to fully experience everything that it is to have a rich and diverse human life.

Equally, we might have peak experiences that are truly not of that everyday human life. Magnificent times, when we realise our full creative potential, and sit temporarily in a place where we feel the constant presence of the Something More flow gently through us. However, our self awareness does not need, or choose, to immerse itself deep in the Something More for most of our life experience.

For the main part, our self awareness simply chooses to get on with living out our human life in our human world and with sharing our co-created human experience together. We choose to spend most of our time experiencing our human world in this very human way because, for the main part, that is the reason why most of us have chosen to experience a human life in the first place.

129

By choosing to live our human life in a very human way, we are able to maintain connection with others who enrich our life experience. We are able to interact with them on their own terms, and encourage them in their endeavours as they too go about exploring their sense of self. By staying with the human world we are able to discharge those practical responsibilities that we have chosen to become such an important part of our everyday life.

In coming to know ourself more deeply, we come to understand that being a part of everyday human life really is what we have chosen for this particular journey. We grow beyond the quest for moments of peak experience, that we hope will transform our identity. Instead we come to know ourself as an entity that flows within, and as an inseparable part of, each and every moment of our everyday life experience.

We come to accept that there is a natural ebb and flow to our sense of connection, to it's depth and to it's intensity. We accept that wherever our self awareness may sit in the moment, be it with our mind, our body or closer to our highest self, life goes on. We are at peace with the fact that we may well go on to create negative or destructive situations at some future date, because that might be what we choose to experience or share with others, at the time. However, we also know that as peace grows within us, so does it blossom in the world around us.

Equally, we come to understand, in our relationship with others, that they too have their ebb and flow. Sometimes they might feel connected and empowered, sometimes they might feel lost and alone. So at different times different people might require very different things from us. Sometimes we might choose to resonate in harmony together and other times we might choose to create discord.

Knowing these things we can forgive ourself, and others, for the times we choose to create a life that is way below our full potential. As we can forgive ourself and others for the challenges that we have shared in the past. We can choose to accept the actions of ourself and others as the inevitable manifestation of whatever our self awareness chooses to experience in the moment. And we can know that each and every one of our choices and each and every one of our experiences is and ever will be, perfect in the moment of it's creation.

Made in the USA
Charleston, SC
05 May 2015